ANGELA LANSBURY:

A BIOGRAPHY

◆

MARGARET WANDER BONANNO

St. Martin's P
New York

Grateful acknowledgment is made for permission to quote from the following:

"Everybody Says Don't" by Stephen Sondheim
Copyright © 1964 by Stephen Sondheim.
All rights administered by Chappell & Co. Inc.
International copyright secured. All rights reserved.
Used by permission.

"It's Today" from *Mame*.
Music and Lyric by Jerry Herman.
Copyright © 1966 Jerry Herman.
All rights controlled by Jerryco Music Co.
Exclusive agent: Edwin H. Morris & Company, A Division of MPL
Communications, Inc.
International copyright secured. All rights reserved. Used by permission.

ANGELA LANSBURY: A BIOGRAPHY
Copyright © 1987 by Margaret Wander Bonanno. All rights reserved. Printed in the
United States of America. No part of this book may be used or reproduced in any
manner whatsoever without written permission except in the case of brief quotations
embodied in critical articles or reviews. For information, address St. Martin's Press,
175 Fifth Avenue, New York, N.Y. 10010

Design by Jessica Winer

Library of Congress Cataloging-in-Publication Data
Bonanno, Margaret Wander.
    Angela Lansbury : a biography.

    1. Lansbury, Angela, 1925–   . 2. Actors—
United States—Biography. I. Title.
PN2287.L2845B6   1987   792'.028'0924   [B]   87–4461
ISBN 0-312-00561-X

First Edition
10 9 8 7 6 5 4 3 2 1

Acknowledgments

I would most especially like to thank the following individuals:

Diana Maychick and Mrs. Rosenthal of the *New York Post*, for permitting me to rummage through the files for three entire days;

Terry Geesken and Mary Corliss of the Museum of Modern Art's Film Stills Archive;

Mr. Donald Fowle and the staff of the Billy Rose Theater Collection of the New York Public Library at Lincoln Center;

My agent, Ted Chichak, for ten years at hard labor, and for saving me from The Black Hole That Ate the Midlist Writer.

Angela Brigid Lansbury . . .

Her grandfather was head of Britain's Labour party, an advocate of women's rights, and a good friend of Mahatma Gandhi.

Her mother was the lovely and lyrical Irish actress Moyna MacGill, her father a prosperous London merchant.

Evacuated from Britain during the blitz, young Angela considered a career in politics before show business began to exert its irresistible lure . . .

Angela Lansbury . . .

Alias Auntie Mame, Mama Rose, Mrs. Lovett, Jessica Fletcher . . .

At sixteen she made her singing debut in a Montreal nightspot.

Before she was twenty she had costarred with Ingrid Bergman and George Sanders and been nominated for two Academy Awards for *Gaslight* and *The Picture of Dorian Gray.*

But for the next twenty years, first as a contract player with Metro-Goldwyn-Mayer, later on her own, she slogged through dozens of "featured" roles, the victim of narrow-minded directors who perversely cast her in parts ten to twenty years older than she really was. She was doomed, in her own words, to "playing bitches on wheels and people's mothers." It was a combination of both that won her a third Oscar nomination for her chilling performance in *The Manchurian Candidate.*

Not content to be "just" a movie actress (she made five films with Metro in a single year), Angela set her sights on Broadway. From the slapstick farce of *Hotel Paradiso* in which she costarred with Bert Lahr, to the grim realism of *A Taste of Honey,* to the whimsy of

1

Stephen Sondheim's ill-fated *Anyone Can Whistle,* she began to make a name for herself. And even when the critics hated the play, they loved Angela.

It wasn't until *Mame* that Angela Lansbury finally came into her own. At the age of forty-one, when most actresses face the harsh reality of being "in-between"—past the age of the ingénue, too young to play character parts—she became an "overnight success" after a quarter of a century of trying.

There would be four Tony Awards, three Golden Globes, and a chance to play Shakespeare at the Old Vic. There would be yet another medium to conquer, television, which in time would bring her the star vehicle "Murder, She Wrote," a consistent top-ten in the Neilsen ratings. There would be homes on both coasts and a dream house in Ireland.

There would also be tragedy. Her Malibu home would be gutted in a brush fire. Her mother Moyna would die a slow and agonizing death from throat cancer. And Angela's two bright, beautiful children would nearly destroy themselves with drugs.

But in the words of another mother she would play in *Gypsy,* Angela "got her kids out." Pulling up stakes and starting a new life in Ireland, she announced she would not set foot onstage again until her children were cured. Everyone thought she had retired.

But she came back, in a revival of *Gypsy* that would send her hometown of London reeling. She wowed them on Broadway yet again, with *Gypsy* and *Mame* and the bizarre comedy of *Sweeney Todd.* And she hasn't slowed down since.

As performer and woman, Angela Lansbury has proven time and again that she can take whatever life dishes out. Like Mame, she's "just sensational," and she keeps on getting better.

> *I was shy, a skirt-hider-behinder. Even when I went to school, other youngsters would say, "There goes what's-her-name."*

*A*re stars born or made? If the little girl born to the Lansbury household in London on October 16, 1925 had come from a more ordinary family, would she herself have been ordinary? Probably not. But coming from a family of overachievers may have given Angela Brigid Lansbury a special boost that other children her age in prewar England didn't have.

The Lansburys were very, very British. They were members of the Church of England and their family had worshipped in the same church for three generations. Both Angela's father and her paternal grandfather had been members of the House of Commons for the borough of Poplar, a suburb of London. Her mother's people, the McIldowies, were Irish.

"I'm eternally grateful for the Irish side of me," Angela says. "That's where I get my sense of comedy and whimsy. As for the English half—that's my reserved side . . . but put me on a stage and the Irish comes out."

The greatest influence on the Irish side was Angela's mother, Moyna MacGill. Born Charlotte Lillian McIldowie, she changed her name to Moyna MacGill before making her London debut in *Dear Brutus* at the age of nineteen. Moyna's was a distinguished theatrical family spanning several generations. Her father, William McIldowie, was director of the Belfast Opera. Her uncle, Robert Mantell, toured America at the turn of the century in such classics as

The School for Scandal and *The Dagger and the Cross*. Until his death in 1928, he and his Shakespearean company trouped from one end of the country to the other, and Mantell always played the title roles in *King Lear* and *Richard III* and *Hamlet*. Two of Moyna's brothers, James and Dennis McIldowie, also trod the boards in London and America.

Studying old photographs, it is easy to see that Angela's looks come from her mother's side. The McIldowies all have the same overlarge, expressive eyes, that same strong jaw and well-defined profile. From the Shakespearean actor Robert Mantell to his grand-niece Angela, the legacy is clear.

Moyna MacGill remained the darling of London play-goers throughout the twenties and thirties, costarring with such luminaries as Basil Rathbone, Herbert Marshall, Philip Merivale, and John Gielgud in the West End. Somehow she also found time for politics, serving as mayoress of Poplar in 1926. She even appeared on Broadway in *Interference* in 1927, when Angela was only two.

Married at first to the distinguished actor/director/playwright Reginald Denham, Moyna had a daughter Isolde, who would also go into the theater. Her marriage from Denham dissolved, Moyna married Edgar Isaac Lansbury, as far a cry from a theatrical personality as one could find.

"My father wasn't in the business at all," Angela says. "But he loved the theater—and adored my mother."

Edgar Lansbury was a successful lumber merchant, one-time mayor of Poplar, and former member of Parliament. A quiet man, he died when Angela was nine, and her memories of him are understandably vague.

Not so her memories of her paternal grandfather. In spite of his being on her "reserved" British side, George Lansbury was quite a character in his own right. If he hadn't been a beloved political leader, he might well have been an accomplished actor.

"He awed me," Angela remembers. "He was a pacifist and a great friend of Gandhi's, six feet tall with muttonchop whiskers."

George Lansbury was a self-made man. Poverty forced him to

leave school and earn a living while still a young boy, and at the age of twenty he became a lifelong socialist. Elected to the House of Commons on the Labour party ticket in 1910, he was asked to resign because of his revolutionary—for those times—support of women's rights.

Pacifism and the needs of the working man (and woman) became George Lansbury's lifelong obsession. He went so far as to resign from the Labour party in 1935 because it voted to support the League of Nations even if it advocated war. A radical to the end, Angela's awesome, bewhiskered grandfather traveled to Russia and throughout Europe, writing several books and pamphlets on his observations of working conditions there. He died in 1940 at the age of eighty-one.

Angela remembers him this way. "He was a giant of my youth because he was in our house all the time and even now in England my name is not known for Angela Lansbury but because I'm George Lansbury's granddaughter."

As late as 1973, when Angela was touring London in *Gypsy* and her grandfather had been dead for more than thirty years, a fan came backstage to show her three bronze medals she had won for netball as a girl, awarded her by the Hon. George Lansbury.

"I was taken to hear him give Labour party speeches," Angela recalls. "When he said 'Friends,' the whole hall just roared with appreciation. At home, I'd get up and give extemporaneous speeches, imitating him."

Consequently even the "non-theatrical" side of her family inspired young Angela's career. If she hadn't been an actress, she admits, she might have gone into politics. But, she says: "I wanted to be an actress from the word 'go.'"

Angela and her half-sister Isolde put on shows to entertain family members. When they were old enough, Angela's twin brothers Bruce and Edgar, five years younger, joined the act. Edgar, now a television and Broadway producer, once played the Big Bad Wolf to Angela's Little Red Riding Hood in a family Christmas pageant. Angela has this to say about her little brother's performance.

"Brother is one hell of a better producer than he ever was an actor in *Little Red Riding Hood*. He simply could not get his fangs together."

"She was a nasty little girl," Edgar jokes, then amends his opinion. "In retrospect I can see now that she was a sweet, kind, considerate sister."

Whatever the truth, and it probably lies somewhere in between, a picture is already emerging of a very complex young lady. In her own assessment she may have been shy, yet she was performing for a select audience almost from the time she could talk. And while her classmates at the South Hampstead High School for Girls might not have remembered her, she was already finding the means to make a name for herself.

At the age of twelve, she sat absolutely mesmerized through three performances of George Bernard Shaw's *Pygmalion* at the Old Vic. Moyna had already made use of her daughter's extraordinary sense of comic timing by teaching her a kind of cabaret act. Angela did impersonations of Wagnerian sopranos and of the zany British comedienne Bea Lillie singing her trademark song, "I Went to a Marvelous Party." She was enrolled at the Webber-Douglas School for Dramatic Arts just before the war. London was an idyllic place in those years.

"The world of the thirties, when I was a child, was such a magical place," Angela reminisces, a trace of her childhood Cockney accent still clinging after all these years. "I miss the old sweet shops where you could get Knickerbocker Glories. You could have a great adventure with a spare sixpence in those days."

But the magic was not to last. Angela was barely into her teens when World War II broke out, and the bombing of London began.

"My mother said, 'Look, you can go to the country to get away from the bombs, or you can stay here.'"

Stay she did. While her school was evacuated to safety in the countryside, Angela remained in London, studying with a private tutor and taking evening classes in diction, dancing, and singing. Meanwhile, her mother was driving an ambulance.

It is possible that Britain might have gone under in those grim, early months of the blitz if it wasn't for the courage and hard work of her women. Many young, single women joined the RAF and related services as nurses and war-room aides. Housewives became factory workers and letter carriers, filling jobs for the men away at the front. Others from every social class became air-raid wardens, and volunteered in hospitals and relief centers throughout London. Edgar Lansbury's widow did her bit.

Often there simply weren't enough ambulances to transport those critically wounded in the nightly bombing during the worst of the Battle of Britain. Milk trucks, delivery vans, even horse-drawn carts were pressed into service, and the volunteers who drove them risked their lives daily. At a time when celebrities like Vivien Leigh and Laurence Olivier were entertaining besieged Londoners in underground stations and air-raid shelters, the woman who had played Desdemona to Basil Rathbone's Othello took a more practical approach. Dodging craters and listening for the deadly whine of the next incoming bomb, Moyna MacGill, the darling of the West End, careened nightly through the blacked-out streets of London saving numerous lives.

But the constant threat of death to her young family was too much even for Moyna. With her elder daughter Isolde's marriage to actor Peter Ustinov, Moyna felt there was no further reason to remain in London. She could take no money out of England. Passage to New York for her and her children was arranged by a group of wealthy American sponsors who engaged her to look after ten refugee children leaving on a later boat. Moyna and her brood—Angela, age fourteen, the twins Bruce and Edgar, age nine—abandoned everything to cross the U-boat infested Atlantic on one of the last ships permitted to leave England.

What must Angela have been thinking on that at once tedious and potentially fatal journey? In her brief life she had watched the city she loved change from a safe, adventure-filled place to a city of rubble and flame and terror. She was leaving the only home she had ever known for an uncertain future in a strange land. She could not possibly have imagined, searching the horizon beyond those treacherous waters, what the New World held in store for her.

I used to walk down 44th Street from the American Theater Wing Stage Door Canteen, where I danced with the GI's, and my head would buzz with excitement at the very thought of what could happen, what one could do. And standing outside Sardi's, it was even more fun than getting in.

New York was a one room apartment, shared with her mum and the boys, at 55 Morton Street in Greenwich Village. New York was a scholarship from the American Theater Wing and classes at the Feagin School for Drama and Radio. New York was a great deal of hard work and few luxuries. But New York was also the continuation of the dream.

Angela remembers walking along Broadway. "The names on the marquees: Helen Hayes, Gladys George, Katherine Cornell and, of course, Judith Evelyn in *Angel Street.*"

Little did the fifteen-year-old realize, staring up at the lights along the Great White Way, that within two years she would make her movie debut in *Gaslight,* the film version of *Angel Street.*

Although it would soon improve, life in America began with hard times. The group of children Moyna had been hired to look after in New York never arrived. A refugee ship, the *City of Benares,* had been torpedoed by a German submarine and seventy people lost their lives. From then on the British government banned all civilian sea traffic until the end of the war. Moyna had left everything behind in England. With no means of employment, she was, as her daughter put it, "hard put to it."

But one of her American sponsors came to the rescue. Charles T. Wilson was a well-to-do Wall Street businessman. He and his wife invited the Lansbury clan to share their home in Lake Mahopac in New York's posh Westchester County.

The Lansburys lived with the Wilsons for a year. Angela commuted daily to the city to continue her theater training at the Feagin School. There she got her first character part, as Lady Wishfort in William Congreve's Restoration comedy *The Way of the World*.

She also continued to polish her cabaret act, the parodies of Bea Lillie and Wagnerian divas Moyna had coached her in as a child. That act was to earn her her first paying job. She was only sixteen, but she was tall, carried herself well, and must have looked older or she would never have been allowed to perform at the Samovar Club in Montreal. After that it all began to happen rather fast.

While Angela was regaling audiences in Montreal, Moyna was also on the move. Touring Canada with a variety show sponsored by the Canadian Air Force, she was selling war bonds in Vancouver, British Columbia when her agent called her from Hollywood. He told her about a role in a movie called *The Commandos Strike At Dawn*. Not letting a little thing like distance bother her, Moyna made the thirteen hundred mile train trip only to find that the role had been taken. Undaunted, she decided then and there that California was a better place for her career and her daughter's. She sent for Angela.

With nothing but a train ticket and twenty dollars for meals, Angela set out for California. But movie roles eluded both mother and daughter.

"I couldn't get a job in the movies," Angela says. "So I got one in a lovely store in Los Angeles called Bullocks-Wilshire."

Bullocks was a department store catering to a Beverly Hills clientele. Angela's starting salary was eighteen dollars a week. She wrapped packages, sold cosmetics and handbags, and later worked her way up to twenty-seven dollars a week. Moyna worked in Bullocks' toy department. Mother and daughter continued to audition for movie roles. Christmas 1942 came and went.

Then Angela got word that Metro-Goldwyn-Mayer had acquired a script for *The Picture Of Dorian Gray,* based on Oscar Wilde's novel about a dissolute young man who never seems to age. The role of Sybil Vane, the tragic music hall singer who loves Dorian, seemed perfect for her. She could sing and dance as well as act creditably in a serious dramatic role. Her agent arranged an audition.

She would eventually get to play Sybil in the film, but it would not be her first role. Instead she had the good fortune to work in her very first movie with the man known as "the woman's director," the director who brought out the best in Hepburn and Crawford and a host of others—George Cukor.

Gaslight was exactly the kind of film George Cukor did best. Based on Patrick Hamilton's stage play *Angel Street,* it is about a murderer who marries his victim's niece in order to claim her inheritance by trying to drive her insane. It had already been filmed in Britain under the title *The Murder In Thornton Square,* starring Anton Walbrook and Diana Wynyard.

The rumor persisted for years that M-G-M had acquired the rights to distribute the British film in America, but that the negative was mysteriously destroyed. However, a pirated version turned up at the National Film Theatre Awards in the sixties, and the film was officially released in this country in 1978.

Metro, however, decided to shoot its own version. Charles Boyer, cast against type as the murderer, with Ingrid Bergman as his unsuspecting wife/victim, under the direction of George Cukor, seemed the ideal combination.

Most critics thought *Gaslight* did not measure up to either its British counterpart or the original theatrical version, which had the advantage of containing all of the action in a one room set, creating

11

an atmosphere of claustrophobia and suspense. But Cukor's use of unusual camera angles and soft lighting created the proper eerie mood. And the original plot was complicated in the American version by a love triangle in which a pretty, conniving maid attempts to lure the murderer away from his wife.

Angela tested for the role of Nancy the maid. Cukor was impressed with her poise, her blue-eyed good looks, her natural Cockney accent. But looking at the test later, he decided she was too young for the role. Angela went back to the toiletries counter at Bullocks convinced that she had lost the part.

But a week later, George Cukor changed his mind. Something about the fetching strawberry-blonde who played older than her age made him have another look at the screen test. He called Angela in for a second audition. Not only did he cast her, he actually had the role of Nancy rewritten and expanded for her.

The first thing Angela did was hand in her resignation at Bullocks. When the manager found out that his best cosmetics salesgirl was leaving, he asked her why. With characteristic British understatement, Angela simply told him she had found a better job.

"Tell me how much they offered you," her boss said. "Maybe we can give you the same or even more."

Imagine his face when Angela told him she was getting a raise in pay from twenty-seven to five hundred dollars a week. On George Cukor's casting her in *Gaslight,* Metro-Goldwyn-Mayer signed her to their standard seven-year contract at five hundred dollars per week.

At 5'8", she was the same height as Ingrid Bergman. Cukor made her wear platform shoes to add to her height and accentuate the scenes in which she had to threaten Bergman, her rival for Charles Boyer's affections.

"I imagine they thought my towering over her would make me more sinister," Angela says.

The young actress's age also got in the way. The shooting of the key scene in which she and Bergman have their confrontation, and Angela as the maid lights a cigarette in defiance of her mistress, had to be postponed for several months. Angela was only seventeen, and neither the social worker nor the teacher assigned to the set would allow her to smoke until after her eighteenth birthday. When the day came, Ingrid Bergman and the cast threw a party for their "baby" right on the Metro sound stage.

And the critics noticed her. With praise for Boyer and Bergman in spite of his overall reservations about the film, *New York Times* critic Bosley Crowther paid the newcomer the compliment of putting her performance on an equal footing with a pair of veterans. "Nice little personal vignettes are interestingly contributed . . . by Joseph Cotten as a stubborn detective, Dame May Whitty, and Angela Lansbury as a maid."

And if that was not enough, her very first movie role would also earn her the first of three Academy Award nominations. *Gaslight* won two Oscars, including one for Ingrid Bergman as Best Actress. Angela was nominated for Best Supporting Actress, losing out to no less a luminary than Ethel Barrymore in *None But The Lonely Heart.* Heady stuff indeed for an actress barely old enough to smoke.

Her next venture with Metro was as Elizabeth Taylor's flighty older sister in the heart-warming *National Velvet.* Enid Bagnold's story of a young girl's love for her horse and her ride to victory, disguised as a boy, in Britain's Grand National Steeplechase was to be the Christmas fare at Radio City Music Hall in 1944. Audiences, especially children, craved this kind of idyllic, escapist fare as the war dragged on for yet another year.

Angela remembers the austerity measures that had her riding a bus instead of a studio car to the Metro lot every morning because of gas rationing. But this was not too much of a hardship for someone who had survived the blitz, and she often rode the bus with child star Margaret O'Brien and her mother.

National Velvet, however, must have been something of a comedown after *Gaslight.* The role of Edwina Brown, Velvet's sister, was hardly a challenge, and the critics scarcely noticed Angela. Elizabeth Taylor was everybody's darling. Angela remembers her as "a tiny little girl with violet eyes."

But contract players in those days of the paternalistic studio system did what they were told, particularly when they were told by the likes of studio boss Louis B. Mayer. And Angela still had her eye on another very special role. The part of Sybil Vane in *The Picture Of Dorian Gray* had still not been cast. Angela pleaded for a screen test with director Albert Lewin.

"Miss Lansbury bounced into my office like a young heifer," was how Lewin described it. "To my mind, she was the farthest thing from what I wanted for the role."

But as with *Gaslight,* Angela tested twice and the second test "took." And, as with *Gaslight,* the character was eventually rewritten to suit the actress.

Angela was cast partly because she fitted the ideal of beauty popular in Oscar Wilde's day. Or at least, as James Agee suggested, the ideal as seen in pornographic prints of the era. With her creamy skin and softly rounded figure, her golden ringlets and big blue eyes, and of course, her lilting singing voice, she projected a kind of tarnished vulnerability that was perfect for Sybil Vane, the music hall singer who charms the decadent Dorian, only to be rejected by him. More than forty years later, audiences who remember nothing else about the picture recall her as "the girl who sang the song about the little yellow bird."

The film itself was a landmark for its time. It was shot entirely in black and white, with one exception. The portrait of Dorian, which shows the effects of age and corruption while Dorian himself remains eternally young, was photographed in Technicolor. It hovered like a specter over the vain young man, revealing the skull beneath the handsome face. The technique was extraordinary for its time, and added to the frightening quality of Oscar Wilde's fantasy as scripted by director Albert Lewin.

Possibly the film was too avant-garde for its era; certainly critics like Bosley Crowther failed to understand it. He thought the film "mawkish," criticized Lewin's pacing as a director, and found Hurd Hatfield "incredibly stiff" in the title role. As for Angela, his remarks were even more cruel.

"Angela Lansbury wears a quaint little costume as a music-hall-singing Sybil Vane and wears an even more ridiculous pose of purity which provokes Dorian's bestiality."

One wonders, however, if Mr. Crowther was truly paying attention. He was inattentive enough to mistake supporting actor George Sanders' off-camera narration as the evil genius Lord Henry Wotten, for the voice of Sir Cedric Hardwicke "sitting sternly in an invisible cloud."

Regardless of the critics, Angela triumphed once again with a second Oscar nomination in less than a year. Once again she lost, this time to Anne Revere, her costar in *National Velvet*.

It must have been disappointing, but Angela had other things on her mind. Among them were the series of films M-G-M had lined up for her in the upcoming year. Another serious consideration was her marriage, to actor Richard Cromwell.

Richard Cromwell, born Roy Radebaugh, was an American actor fifteen years Angela's senior. In *The Filmgoer's Companion*, Leslie Halliwell descibes him as a "leading man, [the] gentle hero of early sound films." He did thirty-nine films, from *Tol'able David* in 1930 through *Lives of A Bengal Lancer*, *Jezebel*, *Young Mr. Lincoln*, *Enemy Agent* and *Parachute Battalion*. He also appeared briefly on Broadway. In early photos he looks like a young Errol Flynn—a fair-haired matinee idol. It's no wonder Angela fell in love with him. The marriage lasted a little over nine months, ending in divorce in 1946.

"He was extremely interesting," Angela says. As to why it went wrong: "I was too young at nineteen. [The marriage] shouldn't have happened."

Dick Cromwell only made a single public statement about one of Angela's bad habits, in an interview with Liza Wilson of *The American Weekly*. "All over the house, tea bags. In the middle of the night she'd get up and start drinking tea. It nearly drove me crazy."

Summing up she said, "[The marriage] was a mistake, but a very good lesson. I wouldn't have *not* done it."

For the next few years she made the round of Hollywood parties, meeting a number of men, mostly in the film industry. But there was no one she was particularly fond of. Part of the problem was the men themselves.

"The Hollywood men are so darned keen on themselves," she told Earl Wilson of the *New York Post* in an interview in 1947. "They don't take a minute out to talk about you. They adore themselves so much, they make love to themselves constantly. When I get married again, I expect to marry somebody who isn't an actor at all."

Her tone may have been slightly bitter following her relationship with Cromwell, but her observations were right on target. Not taken in by the movie star image, she threw herself back into her work and waited for something better to come along.

Five hundred dollars a week was a great deal of money in the late forties, and Metro made certain it got its money's worth out of Angela. In 1946 alone she would appear in five films, none of which would do anything to advance her career or make use of her real talents. In fact, she was typecast for years, trapped in a series of thankless "bad girl" roles. It seemed every time a script called for a tramp or a bitter older woman, Angela was it.

"Certainly in retrospect it is difficult to see why M-G-M kept Lansbury as a featured player while making stars of [Lana] Turner, or June Allyson or Janet Leigh," David Shipman wrote in *The Great Movie Stars*. The sad fact is that Angela very often ended up in support of the aforementioned stars and stole the film out from under them.

Maybe it was because she never played the casting couch game as so many other starlets did. It would have been easy with studio head Louis B. Mayer, a notorious skirt-chaser. But Mayer never chased Angela. He also never gave her the roles she wanted.

As Angela herself once put it, M-G-M "had Esther Williams to swim, Judy Garland to sing, June Allyson to jitterbug, and Lena Horne to lean against pillars." They didn't seem to know what to do with her. All she wanted was the kind of part Jean Arthur played. Or, as she told an interviewer at the time, a role opposite Clark Gable or Jimmy Stewart would have been nice. "Or some other he-man, in which he breaks down the door and I'm behind it. I want to be the reason he broke down the door."

Hollywood never would give her that kind of role, but at least in those early years it kept her busy. Five hundred dollars a week bought an ultramodern house in an area of Beverly Hills known as Uplifters Ranch. It featured a living room with one entire wall made of glass to show off the fantastic view of the surrounding hills, and a pushbutton bar that popped up out of the floor on its own little elevator. Angela's roommates included a cat named Ingrid (after Ingrid Bergman) and a dog named Fellah who slept at the foot of her bed. The whole family was busy. Bruce and Edgar were attending classes at U.C.L.A. Angela and her mother were making movies.

Moyna had appeared in small cameo roles in two of her daughter's films, *National Velvet* and *The Picture of Dorian Gray*. Directors chose her whenever they needed "a middle-aged Englishwoman of distinguished appearance." Her next film was *Uncle Harry*, with George Sanders (late of *Dorian Gray*, and with whom Angela would work in *The Private Affairs of Bel Ami* later in the year), and costarring Geraldine Fitzgerald and Ella Raines. Angela, meanwhile, got a chance to rough up Judy Garland.

"People hissed me in public for being mean to Judy in *The Harvey Girls*," Angela recalls. She made it look that real.

The Harvey Girls was a pleasant piece of fluff, a musical about a group of traveling waitresses who followed the Santa Fe railroads into western frontier towns. The Harvey Girls represented clean tablecloths and clean living. In contrast to them were the girls in John Hodiak's saloon. Angela was one of them.

An exuberant song-and-dance movie whose star-studded cast included Ray Bolger, Preston Foster, Virginia O'Brien, Kenny Baker and Marjorie Main, *The Harvey Girls* is remembered today only for the Harry Warren/Johnny Mercer song "On the Atchison, Topeka and Santa Fe," which left audiences humming it for weeks. The "good triumphs over evil plot," in which Angela as a honky-tonk singer loses John Hodiak to the virtuous Judy Garland seems rather silly now. It did garner Angela good reviews, however.

"Angela Lansbury, pouty and pomaded, looks dazzling as the queen of the den," Bosley Crowther wrote, also praising the Technicolor film for its "abundance of chromatic spectacle and an uncommonly good musical score."

There is an ironic final note to *The Harvey Girls.* Johnny Mercer's songs for the movie were later recorded, with most of the original cast. Except for Angela. Her numbers were dubbed in by Virginia Rees.

"In Hollywood they thought I had a reedy little voice," remembers the same star who was to carry roles like Mame and Rose Lee and Anna in *The King and I.* But having her talents largely unappreciated was to become a recurring theme in her years with M-G-M.

Losing her man to another woman was another recurring theme in the films Angela did for Metro. William Powell in *The Hoodlum Saint* was the next to go, lost to Esther Williams, who for once wore street clothes instead of a bathing suit.

The Hoodlum Saint was the story of a hardened newspaperman whose life is changed by the inspiration of St. Dismas, the "good thief" who was crucified at the same time as Jesus. The title is somewhat misleading; some M-G-M executive must have decided that the juxtaposition of words like hoodlum and saint would intrigue audiences enough to make them buy tickets even if they had no idea what the movie was about.

That kind of thinking seems to have affected the entire movie, whose "tediously involved plot, unwieldy dialogue, pat situations, and flat characterizations," in the words of one critic, "add up to a somewhat jumbled and tepid drama."

Angela, playing a torch singer who carries her torch for William Powell, says to him in an early scene, "Isn't it sort of risky to be fooling around with religion?" Possibly someone should have asked the film's producers the same question. At any rate, Angela got a chance to sing once again. *The New York Times's* A.H. Weiler didn't think she had a "reedy little voice."

"Angela Lansbury, as the other woman in [William Powell's] life, is fetching and sings two dated ballads well."

The Private Affairs Of Bel Ami seemed at first to be a chance to break out of the "featured actress" trap. Gintilde de Marelle was yet another loose woman, but the script offered Angela some room to stretch her range. And being based on a novel by Guy de Maupassant lent the movie a little class. Angela was loaned out to United Artists for *Bel Ami*. Albert Lewin, who had directed her in *Dorian Gray,* requested her specifically.

"This is the history of a scoundrel," begins the narration of the film. "The time is eighteen eighty, the place is Paris." De Maupassant's George Duroy, the *bel ami* of the title, is a wastrel and a brute, a man who uses women and casts them aside, throwing off lines like "Love and marriage are two entirely different subjects," and, having made yet another conquest, "I have just lighted a fire in an old soot-filled chimney."

George Sanders, an old acquaintance from *Dorian Gray,* had the title role. Angela played the woman to whom he always returns. In New York for the picture's premiere, she told an interviewer, "You see, he's rather a terrible person in a way. He is always marrying for money. At the end he's about to marry Ann Dvorak. He's still in love with me, and I always know that." Referring to her own role, she said, "It's an unusual part. I think it's rather an unusual picture, too."

The critics thought otherwise. They found *Bel Ami* boring and full of clichés, and blasted its theme of brutalization of women.

Bosley Crowther, in a rare display of sympathy for the performers, placed the blame on the script and the director for giving the actors nowhere to go.

"Ann Dvorak, Angela Lansbury, Katherine Emery—the whole lot of them—are as utterly artificial as the obvious paint-and-pasteboard sets . . . The whole list of love-laden ladies and fancifully costumed gents acts as posily and pompously as they are compelled to talk."

The film also earned Angela an unfortunate nickname. In the publicity stills released for the film, she is shown lying on the floor clutching George Sanders' leg to prevent him from leaving her yet again. The poster earned her the name "The Clutch." It was to haunt her for years.

Till The Clouds Roll By was M-G-M's version of the life of songwriter Jerome Kern, a musical extravaganza with Robert Walker playing Kern and a cast of some of the biggest names and about-to-be-names in the business. Near the bottom of the credits was Angela, along with Frank Sinatra, June Allyson, Lena Horne, Cyd Charisse, and Gower Champion. She sang "How'd You Like to Spoon with Me?" and promptly disappeared in this overblown cavalcade of stars. Most reviews did not even mention her.

Her last film for Metro in 1946 was *Tenth Avenue Angel,* a sticky-sweet vehicle for little Margaret O'Brien. Angela played a schoolteacher to the too-precious slum child, whom John Douglas Eames in *The M-G-M Story* describes as "a little angel of the New York tenements, infecting everyone but the audience with her faith and joy." The film went through endless rewrites, retakes, and recasting, and was not released until eighteen months after its start date. It is scarcely worth mentioning, except that it exists and Angela was in it.

Somehow in the midst of this hectic schedule, Angela found time for a private life. It was very private, not at all the kind of thing most young Hollywood starlets did with their free time. While she did attend the obligatory round of parties and premieres—and loved them—she was primarily a homebody. A fanatical cook, she preferred eating at home to dining out, preparing her own steak-and-kidney pie, artichoke salad, and "the best cheesecake in Hollywood—the real kind, not the pinup variety," as she joked with columnist Earl Wilson, who described her at age twenty as being "pretty as an apartment lease."

At this age she was a chain-smoker, mostly to keep her weight down, which was always a bit of a problem. She was passionately fond of tea, drank the hard stuff in moderation, enjoyed good after-dinner conversation, and a few hands of bridge. She considered herself a whiz at gin rummy.

She was also a reader, quite a rarity in Tinsel Town then or now. Her favorite author was F. Scott Fitzgerald, her favorite book *The Golden Age*. She was brash enough to admit she read for enjoyment—not because she was looking for roles.

The overall picture is of a very mature young lady. But she was by no means stuffy. She played tennis, rode horseback, was a fair watercolorist, and admitted to a weakness for flattery, autograph hunters, and dominant men. "I like food, period. I like men, period," she said in an interview.

She tended toward pale blue silk nightgowns in winter, slept nude in summer, wore slacks and sweaters and no makeup at home and only dressed up to go out. She seemed content with her life at this point, neither impatient about the course her career was taking, nor about the quietness of her social life. "I'm the lettuce type," was how she put it. "I'm not at all moody. I'm very placid and dogmatic."

It was perhaps just as well for her career, which would consist of more of the same for years. But her social life was about to undergo a radical change.

Angela had been divorced from Dick Cromwell for about a year when she was invited to a housewarming party at the home of Hurd Hatfield, her costar in *The Picture of Dorian Gray*. Hatfield lived in the Ojai Valley, some fifty miles northwest of Los Angeles. When Angela said she didn't have a ride Hatfield arranged one for her. He had a friend, a young Irish-born theatrical designer, who would take her in his car. The friend was Peter Pullen Shaw.

Peter Shaw had started out in Hollywood as an actor under contract to M-G-M. But he couldn't get work because producers thought he looked too much like Errol Flynn or Tyrone Power, and they already had them. Peter became a theatrical designer instead.

It was a good thing he abandoned acting or Angela might never have given him a second look. Her marriage to Cromwell had soured her on actors for good. "I'm glad he's not an actor," she says of Peter. "I'm sure we'd get into fights if he were. I can't bear fights. Some

23

people fight to make up. I don't want that as a basis for a relationship."

It was a long drive to the party, and doubtless the two young people found a great deal to talk about—their shared Irish roots and their respective careers in "the industry." They began to see each other regularly after that, but Angela was careful of her privacy, describing Peter to a curious columnist as "just a dining and dancing friend."

Privacy was essential. Each of them had been hurt before. Peter was also divorced, and had custody of his small son. Neither he nor Angela needed the glare of publicity to endanger their fragile, growing friendship.

"We had a very slow sort of courtship," Angela remembers. "Peter had a little boy, David, and I'd been burnt. We didn't get married until two years later."

Their carefully nurtured romance was to blossom into an enduring love. This time, each knew, it was forever. Angela and Peter set about planning a wedding that would show the world how they felt about each other.

They decided to be married in England. Since her grandfather's day the Lansburys had worshipped in the Bow Street Church not far from where Angela was born. In May of 1949, the couple announced their plans to marry in Angela's ancestral church.

They arrived in London in July. About forty guests were expected to arrive later. Moyna was on her way, along with Bruce and Edgar, who would decide by flipping a coin which of them was to give the bride away. Angela had brought her wedding dress with her, a beautiful gown of rose taffeta and Chantilly lace. The wedding was going to be perfect.

It almost didn't happen. The vicar of the Bow Street Church, the Reverend G.F.J. Ansell, refused to marry the couple, saying he "could not find it in my conscience to marry someone in my church who has been married before." Official Church of England policy forbids marriages between divorced persons, but the final decision is usually left to the bishop of each diocese. An exception could easily

24

have been made in this case, and one can't help wondering if the vicar was looking for a little public attention.

Whether he was or not, public attention was exactly what Vicar Ansell got. No less a voice than the London *Daily Express* denounced his decision as "callous and cruel," pointing out that Miss Lansbury had flown six thousand miles to be married in her grandfather's church. In an editorial in the *Express,* the distinguished Lord Beaverbrook took issue with the vicar and his Church.

"As years roll on the Church of England makes no change, no alteration, no variation at all in rules which belong to the dark ages. Thereby it forfeits leadership among the young people it should love and cherish."

But the vicar held firm, and Angela and Peter set about looking for another church in the Cockney section near Bow Street. Both the superintendent of Whitechapel Methodist Mission and the pastor of the Deptford Congregational Church offered their services. But it was the Church of Scotland's St. Columba's which finally had the honor.

The Church of Scotland's philosophy with regard to remarriage is almost identical with the Church of England's. But the Reverend R. F. V. Scott, who ultimately wed the couple, did not know of the publicity surrounding their run-in with the Bow Street vicar.

"I went to Norway for a holiday on July 14 and did not return until last Saturday," the Reverend Scott told a reporter from the New York *Herald Tribune* a week before the wedding. "And I did not see an English paper during that time."

Having promised to perform the wedding for the couple, the Reverend Dr. Scott said, "I cannot go back on my word to them."

Finally, on August 12, 1949, Angela became Mrs. Peter Shaw in St. Columba's Presbyterian Church in the arty Chelsea section of London. Angela wore her rose taffeta gown, with a garland of roses and orange blossoms in her red-gold hair. Nearly two hundred people witnessed the ceremony; forty were the invited guests, the rest were well-wishers who stood on the pavement outside.

"The bride was given away by her brother Edgar, 20," the New

York *Post* reported, "who tossed a coin with his twin, Bruce, for the privilege. Miss Lansbury did *not* promise to obey."

Whatever Angela did or did not promise, the relationship works. One good reason is that, for Angela, her family has always come first.

"Without Peter and the children I feel like half a pair of scissors," she said during one of her biggest triumphs, the run of *Mame* in 1966. "Without this other part of my life the theater is very hollow for me."

It was this attitude that helped her and Peter survive the horrors of their children's drug problems in the early seventies. Together they have survived the rollercoasters of both their careers. Each knows what's best for the other, and part of the reason Peter has been Angela's manager and business partner for the past thirteen years is his deep understanding of what makes this lady tick.

"We have a marvelous relationship," Angela sums it up. "So comfortable with each other, and so in love with one another, which is wonderful after all these years."

> *Someone decided I should be the youngest character actress in the business. I never had the chocolate-box looks they wanted for romantic leads in those days. So when I was in my twenties, I was in makeup to play beastly women in their forties and fifties.*

*T*he spate of beastly women Angela would play began with Mabel Sabre in *If Winter Comes,* the film version of A.S.M. Hutchinson's melodramatic novel about the destructive effects of gossip in a small English village. The 1947 M-G-M version was a remake of the 1923 original, updated for Walter Pidgeon as Mark Sabre, the quiet, un-assuming textbook editor who is destroyed by the wagging tongues of his neighbors, and Deborah Kerr as his old flame. A very young Janet Leigh had a touching role as a village girl fallen on hard times whom the professor tries to help, thereby hastening his destruction. Angela got the role of his bitter, unattractive, and suspicious wife.

Strangely, she was cast because director Victor Saville had been impressed with her performance as Sybil in *Dorian Gray.* It is hard to find two screen characters who are further apart either in age or in temperament than Sybil Vane and Mabel Sabre. Twenty-two-year-old Angela was aged nearly fifteen years to *look* middle-aged, but it was sheer professional acting technique that created the illusion of *being* thirty-five. In his review, Thomas M. Pryor of the *New York Times* remarked, "Angela Lansbury is quite believable and proper as the distrusting wife."

Her next film, *State Of The Union,* was to age her even more. This film was one of the series of Spencer Tracy/Katharine Hepburn vehicles that was to immortalize one of Hollywood's most dynamic screen couples. The contrast between the New England schoolmarm and the streetwise Irishman made for magical screen chemistry. But originally Katharine Hepburn was not in *State Of The Union* at all.

The role of Grant Matthews, the Wendell Willkie-like industrialist who decides to run for president on an idealistic liberal platform, had always been intended for Spencer Tracy. But Claudette Colbert was originally cast as Matthews' wife. When Miss Colbert started making impossible demands on the first day of shooting, director Frank Capra fired her right on the set. The entire film might have gone down the tubes right there if the redoubtable Kate Hepburn hadn't stepped in.

The role of the embittered newspaperwoman who at first supports Matthews and then sets out to destroy him was a risky bit of casting. Capra had seen Angela in *If Winter Comes* and might not have been aware of how young she was. He called her long distance from New York to ask her to consider the role of Kay Thorndyke.

Their first encounter must have been a shock for Capra. Into his Hollywood office bounced this sweet-looking, big-eyed girl, complete with a pink ribbon in her hair. Was it possible to turn her into a hard-edged, worldly-wise forty-five-year-old political pundit? Frank Capra was known as a risk-taker—the very subject matter of the film in those McCarthyite days, not to mention his handling of the Colbert situation was proof of that—but had he overreached himself this time?

"All of us, including Mr. Capra, had our fingers crossed on the role," Angela recalls. "And I think we barely squeezed by."

The film was considered highly controversial, and Bosley Crowther among others suggested that the Truman Administration might take exception to its "name-naming candor . . . It makes no bones about it—the villains of this piece are the 'old Harding gang' politician and a horde of Republican lame-ducks." But President Harry Truman became enamored with the film, showing it over and over again aboard the presidential yacht. Some sources say it even inspired him to run for another term.

While sounding a cautionary note, the critics were essentially approving of *State Of The Union,* although Angela came under their fire for something that was not her fault—her age again. Once again she was playing a bad girl trying to lure a morally-upright man away from his wife, only this time the "girl" she played was twice her age. Bosley Crowther took her to task.

"It is slightly incredible that a lady of such obvious youth and immaturity as Angela Lansbury could make a wised-up Spencer Tracy jump through hoops, which is what she does in this story as the peak in the antique triangle."

The critics' cynicism notwithstanding, Angela was beginning to garner herself some notice in the Hollywood community. While she lost the Oscar for *Dorian Gray,* she did win the Golden Globe Award for Best Supporting Actress. And in 1948, the year she was in *State Of The Union,* Quigley Publications chose her as one of their "Stars of Tomorrow," along with Jane Powell, Cyd Charisse, Ann Blyth, Celeste Holm, Robert Ryan, Jane Peters, Mona Freeman, Eleanor Parker, and Doris Day.

And some columnists were perceptive enough to see her for what she really was. "Hollywood film producers are finding their attention drawn these days to a young Londoner, Angela Lansbury, who is exhibiting on the screen a mixture of charm and authority generally found only in a Churchill speech," Phil Koury, columnist for the *New York Times*, wrote in 1949. "Fans who have been caught up by Miss Lansbury's special brand of radiation may be more than mildly surprised to learn that she is only twenty-three, an age that doesn't fit in at all with the glacial composure, the delicate and ruthless reality that has managed to get into certain of her characterizations."

Koury also saw the handwriting on the wall as far as Angela's future in films was concerned. "Hollywood's love of repetition being what it is, Angela will have to put up with the spate of oldish, adderish portrayals until some astute producer discovers what most observers already concede: that here indeed is a versatile and exciting screen personality."

Despite Angela's efforts to overcome the age difference and give a credible performance in *State Of The Union,* she was not to find that "astute producer" in Louis B. Mayer, who remained blind to her abilities. Angela pleaded with him for an opportunity to play Milady DeWinter in the upcoming remake of *The Three Musketeers.* Mayer ignored her pleas, casting her in the smaller, less challenging role of Queen Anne.

Possibly one of the most frequently remade movies in American film history, *The Three Musketeers* has gone through ten separate reincarnations, from Thomas Edison's 1911 silent through the 1973 extravaganza with Richard Chamberlain as D'Artagnan, the swashbuckling "fourth musketeer" fighting for king and country in seventeenth-century France. Probably the most well-known is the 1921 Douglas Fairbanks remake; possibly the most unusual was the 1939 musical version starring Don Ameche and featuring the Ritz Brothers.

The 1948 Metro version starred Gene Kelly as an acrobatic and appealing D'Artagnan, with Lana Turner in the role Angela had wanted, Milady DeWinter, and featuring a star-studded cast. No effort was made to pretend that this multi-million dollar confection was an intellectual interpretation of the Dumas novel. As Bosley Crowther, entering into the spirit of the film, said:

"More glittering swordplay, more dazzling costumes, more colors or more of Miss Turner's chest have never been seen in a picture than are shown in this one. For those who enjoy a surfeit of such flashy and fleshy displays, there isn't the slightest question that here is a heaping dish."

There is also not the slightest question that it was Lana Turner's chest, not her acting ability, that put her in the spotlight. Angela, by far the better actress, had to content herself with what scene-stealing she could manage as King Louis' extravagant princess.

The studio system that dominated Hollywood in the forties and fifties certainly had its flaws. It locked actors into seven-year contracts and froze their salaries, although at an admittedly high level. It gave them little control over their artistic lives. Studio executives cast themselves as either well-meaning father figures or absolute dictators, whichever was more effective. Either way they treated actors as talented but rather helpless children. Their thinking seemed to parallel Zero Mostel's in Mel Brooks' zany movie *The Producers*. "Actors aren't people . . . have you ever eaten with one?"

But the studio system had one advantage for actors. It guaranteed them work as long as they were under contract and obeyed the rules. And it created a kind of built-in repertory company, where the same actors would often have the opportunity to work together in several films.

Angela had worked with Walter Pidgeon and Janet Leigh in *If Winter Comes*. Later that year she was to have a second opportunity, in *The Red Danube*. She would also appear on the same screen with a living legend of both theater and film—Ethel Barrymore.

The Red Danube was a self-conscious Cold War drama based on Bruce Marshall's novel *Vespers In Vienna* about a young Russian ballerina (Janet Leigh) seeking refuge with the Mother Superior (Ethel Barrymore) of a convent in the British-run sector of postwar Vienna. To return to the Russian sector would mean prison camp and almost certain death. It was a stiff, talky picture in which Ethel Barrymore and Walter Pidgeon (as an agnostic British colonel) spent entirely too much time arguing about religion and morality.

But despite the film's talkiness, Angela's role as Pidgeon's British aide won her favorable critical notice. "Angela Lansbury is fetching as Senior Subaltern Audrey Quail," a critic for the *Times* wrote.

The role also won her the notice of Cecil B. DeMille, who wanted her for his biblical blockbuster, *Samson and Delilah*.

"I feel sorry for actors who never worked with him," Angela says of DeMille. "He was an experience. Taught me how to throw a javelin. Twenty-five yards and I can still hit a bull's-eye."

Likewise, DeMille respected and admired Angela. During shooting, he commented to a reporter about Angela's particular radiant quality. "Some folks use raw alcohol to get warmth and Dutch courage. We have Angela."

Everyone involved with *Samson and Delilah* was to feel some of that special Lansbury radiance, the self-assured glow of a professional who knows her job, takes no nonsense, but at the same time doesn't need to act like a "star." Angela's natural warmth was even commented on by that most jaded of groups, the technicians. "Angela is really lighting up the joint," quipped one of the stage electricians.

And she finally got a chance to play someone close to her own age. The Philistine beauty Semadar, Delilah's sister, was twenty-four in the script. Angela was twenty-three. For once her natural beauty is not smothered under layers of makeup and dowdy clothing. She is stunning in this film, an easy rival for Hedy Lamarr's Delilah. And it is that rivalry, her attempt to steal Samson from Delilah, that earns her an untimely death, speared to a wall in one of the movie's climactic scenes.

"People ask me to this day if it hurt," Angela says.

"As the woman of Timnath, Angela Lansbury is a plump and pouting doll," Bosley Crowther wrote.

The film made no pretense at being true to the orginal biblical story. "Hokum," Roy Pickard called it in *The Oscar Movies From A-Z*. And the *Times'* critic remarked, "Mr. DeMille, that veteran geni who has already engineered three quasi-religious film pageants that tower in the annals of the screen, has here led his carpenters and actors and costumers and camera crews into the vast manufacture of a spectacle that out-Babels anything he's done."

Screenwriters Jesse Lasky Jr. and Frederic M. Frank took extraordinary liberties with the original "script," adding a love story between Samson and Semadar, Angela's character, in order to spice things up a little. It is Delilah's jealousy toward her sister, and her later attempt to avenge Semadar's violent death, that make her a far nobler character in DeMille's film than she ever was in the Bible. But it's hard to imagine Hedy Lamarr as just another scheming loose woman. And no one has ever expected authenticity from the "Bible According to Hollywood." Bosley Crowther summed it up this way. "There are more flowing garments in this picture, more chariots, more temples, more peacock plumes, more animals, more pillows, more spear-carriers, more beards and more sex than ever before . . . if ever there was a movie for DeMillions, here it is."

The very fact that Angela was able to hold her own in this cast of thousands, much less attract the critics' notice, proves that the radiance the cast and crew experienced on the set could also project itself off the screen and affect an audience. One wonders what she might have brought to the film if *she* had played Delilah.

Angela was to do three more films with Metro before her contract expired. She would also have the energy to take time out to have two children in less than two years, and to do summer stock and live television back in New York. It was just as well. She was beginning to get lost in the shuffle. Her name came up less often when new projects were discussed, and her future in films was beginning to look rather dim.

> *I've always done two types of things: first, things like* The Harvey Girls *and* Harlow, *which I could do with my hands tied behind my back, but which appealed to huge masses of people. And second, roles which taxed me emotionally and physically and broke my heart with pride, but only appealed to a small, rather special audience. Roles like Annabel in* All Fall Down *and that heartbreaking woman in* Dark At The Top Of The Stairs *. . . Frankly I wish I had spent more time with my family and less time making mediocre movies in those days.*

Maybe Metro just happened to have a lot of maid costumes in her size. Whatever the reason, six years after her memorable role in *Gaslight*, Angela once again found herself in black dress and frilly white apron, duster in hand, Cockney accent polished off and good as new. The role this time was as the evil Mrs. Edwards in *Kind Lady*, a remake of Hugh Walpole's potboiler about a pack of con artists holding a trusting elderly dowager hostage in an attempt to separate her from her worldly goods.

The plot centers around a winsome artist/con man (Maurice Evans) who wheedles his way into the household of the "kind lady" of the title (Ethel Barrymore), along with a number of impoverished "relatives." Gradually the lady's valuables start to disappear, and she finds herself a prisoner in her own home. The villains are eventually done in by their own evil of course, but the process, and the chance to watch some marvelous performances by the likes of Keenan Wynn and a once more aged-to-fit-the-role Angela, are worth the price of admission.

Kind Lady had originally been a stage play, of the type critic A.H. Weiler called "literate melodrama, impeccably translated by a fine cast." Critics traditionally hate remakes, but they were positive about this one, possibly because the cast included Barrymore and Evans, two veteran Shakespeareans who made movie acting look effortless. Of the supporting cast, Weiler said, "Angela Lansbury and several others make viewing a pleasure. Keenan Wynn and Angela Lansbury, as Evans' muscular and callous Cockney partners in crime . . . assist with fine supporting portrayals."

An astute observer may also notice Moyna MacGill in the small role of Mrs. Harkley. M-G-M got its money's worth out of mother and daughter in this film. Moyna had not been idle in those early Hollywood years. She did several films for Metro, including *Green Dolphin Street,* a piece of exotica about a Maori uprising, complete with fake jungles and studio-tank earthquakes. At the opposite extreme, she was also in *Three Daring Daughters,* a Jeanette Mac-Donald/Jane Powell song and dance confection.

Angela, meanwhile, finished *Kind Lady* and went back to New York, for the first time since the Greenwich Village days, to try her hand at television.

The small screen was still in its infancy in the early fifties. Many of the best shows were shot in the New York area, and most were still done live. Unlike film, where mistakes or bad readings can be corrected by retakes, live television was very much like theater. As in theater, if an actor went up on a line or missed a cue, if a stage prop or piece of scenery refused to cooperate, both veterans and newcomers had to learn to wing it. The only difference was that the theater audience was replaced by a camera and crew. Any actor will confirm that these are the most critical audiences of all.

One of the specialties of the Golden Age of television was the so-called "dramatic anthology." These consisted usually of original stories, or of plays adapted for the new medium of television, performed by an ever-changing repertory of big-name actors as well as newcomers. Today the cast list of any one of these shows would read like a performers' *Who's Who*. Almost every actor of a certain generation got a start in one or several of these dramas. They featured classics like *A Farewell To Arms* and *Dr. Jekyll And Mr. Hyde* and Broadway favorites like *Dinner At 8,* as well as scripts written exclusively for television by such up and coming writers as Rod Serling, whose "Requiem For A Heavyweight" is an example of the best of that era. Some series, like "Screen Directors' Playhouse," in which Angela was to star in 1956, were able to snare "name" Hollywood directors like John Ford, Alfred Hitchcock, and Fred Zinnemann.

Angela's television career began with "Robert Montgomery Presents," one of the bigger budgeted dramas, which was introduced by actor/director/producer Montgomery who sometimes starred in the night's performance.

All told, Angela would appear in some twenty-one of these dramatic anthologies between 1950 and 1959, including an adaptation of Somerset Maugham's *A String of Beads,* with Joan Caulfield and Tom Drake, for the "Schlitz Playhouse of Stars." She also starred in two summer replacement series.

One was the popular "Pantomime Quiz," a classy game show based on the old parlor game of charades, in which two teams of performers competed with each other in acting out famous phrases, literary quotes, etc. Again, the list of regulars and guests reads like a *Who's Who.* Hans Conreid, Vincent Price, Jackie Coogan, Elaine Stritch, Carol Burnett, Dick Van Dyke, Robert Stack, Orson Bean, John Carradine and others shared with Angela the fun of being like a child again in front of a camera and a TV audience.

In equally stellar company, Angela also appeared in "Star Time Playhouse," a dramatic anthology which featured only original stories. Among her peers were Peter Lorre, Basil Rathbone, Broderick Crawford, and Ronald Reagan. In this male-dominated, heavily dramatic series, Angela was the only woman to have star billing throughout one summer's run. Her present success in "Murder, She Wrote" is no fluke, no lucky break for a newcomer, but yet another credit in the repertory of a veteran.

Her fifteenth film was *Mutiny,* an unassuming yarn about the War of 1812, in which Angela, costarring with Mark Stevens and a virtually all male cast played what one critic called "a vicious and dangerous woman." Metro had had nothing to offer her that year, so she was loaned out to United Artists for *Mutiny,* her last venture before embarking on an entirely new career—motherhood.

Helping Moyna raise the twins had been Angela's first exposure to child rearing. "I was an old lady at ten," she recalls. "When my father died, I became the partner with my mother in bringing up my brothers. I had to grow up fast."

She had taken on the responsibility for Peter's small son David when they'd married. Now she and Peter decided to begin a family together. Anthony Peter Shaw was born early in 1952. His sister, Deirdre Angela, was born eighteen months later.

In a generation when most women had to choose between a family and a career, Angela managed to have both. Only someone who has survived the bittersweet experience of young motherhood while trying to juggle a career can appreciate the special kind of heroism this requires. Acting wasn't the kind of settled, stay-in-one-place job where a young mother could take a day off to nurse a sick child or visit a teacher if there was a problem in school. The struggle to maintain a private life and give her children the attention and quality time they needed, while pursuing a career of what she calls "nomadic wandering" between Hollywood and New York in search of work, was to haunt Angela all the years of her children's growing up.

No matter what else was happening in their lives, she and Peter always made time for the children. When they bought their "Japanese house" on a cliff overlooking the beach at Malibu, it was with the children in mind. The secluded spot offered privacy, an essential for the children of any celebrity, as well as the wide open spaces of sea and sky that would help them grow up strong and healthy. Angela wanted her children's lives to be free of the pressures and poverty of her London childhood.

When the children were small, family outings and picnics were the order of the day. These were no mere weenie roasts in the sand, either. Angela was a fanatical cook, and while her beach outings included the standard hot dogs, hamburgers, and marshmallows, the outings also featured the children's favorite dishes, prepared at home to be enjoyed on the beach later. An interview in New York during the run of *A Taste Of Honey* included Angela's recipe for cold chicken, a perennial picnic favorite. Sawed-off card tables with cheery checkered tablecloths, Oriental mats and backrests, and even ice-cream cakes packed in dry ice for the children's birthdays completed the picture of cosy family get-togethers.

In contrast to the movie star's house Angela had bought with her first money from M-G-M, the house in Malibu was at once stylish and very homey. She and Peter called it the "Japanese house" at first because the decor was mostly Hollywood-Oriental when they purchased it. In the style of Frank Lloyd Wright, built all on one level three hundred feet above the beach, it featured sliding glass doors and a fireplace in every room. But it took Angela's particular touch to make it home.

The end result was, in her words, "part Japanese, part California, part Old English." Over the years she and Peter collected old Spanish chests and Florentine paintings and managed to warm up what would otherwise have been a cold, sterile place. But the important thing was not the house so much as its inhabitants. Angela gave the house heart. Family activities always centered around the kitchen.

"I was raised in a kitchen and that's where we gathered at home. I think homes should all be built with up to seventeen suites spoking out from the kitchen. That's where you can talk. Kitchen conversations would reduce juvenile delinquency."

If she could have foreseen the future, she might have heard the irony in that last statement. But when her children were small the horrors of drug abuse in Malibu were only a rumor. And the rumor had not yet touched her family.

She was a good mother, dedicated to a fault, though by her own admission she tended to be "oversolicitous," trying to spare her children some of life's disappointments.

"I'm not a professional mother. I don't bring my kids up by the book," she once told a reporter. "I feel that they're individuals, and I try to treat them as such."

Try she did, but the demands of her career made it impossible to be with her children as often as she wanted. There were several reasons for this.

Conditions at Metro had been less than ideal for her even before Anthony was born. Louis B. Mayer had retired as head of M-G-M, to be replaced by Dore Schary, whose entire philosophy toward running a major studio was different. About the only thing the two men seemed to have in common was utter indifference to promoting Angela's career.

Her contract with Metro expired following *Remains To Be Seen,* and was not renewed. This meant that for the first time since coming to Hollywood, Angela was on her own. The hustle for film and television work would occupy much of her time and energy through most of the fifties.

Though she tried to do fewer films and concentrate on television, so she could fly into New York, shoot a segment of "G.E. Theatre" or "Studio 57" in a day, then quickly fly home to be with her family and tend the roses, the endless commuting must have been wearying. And there were monetary considerations as well.

Her husband Peter had gone through a career change, joining the William Morris Agency as an actors' agent. Mortgages in Malibu were as outrageously high then as they are now. As a Metro contract player earning five hundred dollars a week, Angela had been spoiled. Abandoned by the studio, she felt it incumbent upon her to preserve the family's comfortable lifestyle. That meant a constant search for work.

When she could be with the children, she was with them one hundred and ten percent. When she could not, a young governess, Miss Fyffe, looked after Anthony and Deirdre. Angela remembers her as "a second mother to them."

Broadway first beckoned with *Hotel Paradiso* in 1957. Anthony was five, Deirdre four. When it looked as if the show would have a good long run, Angela realized she could not possibly be separated from her family for months at a time. Anthony, Deirdre and their governess came to live with her in a Manhattan sublet, with Peter commuting from the west coast whenever possible. The Shaws even rented a summer home in Connecticut, with Angela's stepson David joining them for an idyllic summer.

The children followed Angela on location frequently over the years, though it wasn't always the ideal arrangement. As they got older, it meant leaving friends behind in California, changing schools, developing a sense of rootlessness. Angela was torn by the Catch-22 of a career that supported her family and at the same time kept her apart from them. If she left them behind in California, she missed them and worried that she was neglecting them. If she brought them with her to New York or on location in Europe as she did in their teen-age years, she risked disrupting their lives. There seemed to be no perfect solution.

> *Even though I played some very small parts, they always had quality . . . As a character actor I achieved two things. First, a healthy sense of my off-screen self and my private life, which I learned to keep separate from my screen characters. And second, a longevity of career that has outlasted many of the leading ladies who relied on their looks.*

*B*y the summer of 1952, the studio had nothing to offer Angela, so she was released to do summer stock in upstate New York. She did *Affairs Of State* and the Howard Lindsay/Russell Crouse thriller *Remains To Be Seen* in repertory on the straw hat circuit for the entire summer. Someone at Metro had the brilliant idea that *Remains To Be Seen* would make a good movie. It was Angela's final project before her contract expired.

In the hands of some M-G-M genius, this quickie celluloid version of the Lindsay/Crouse mystery became a "comedy thriller" with music. June Allyson, Van Johnson, and Dorothy Dandridge sing, and Johnson plays the drums. Whenever he does, Angela, as the sinister villainess of the piece, comes out of the panels in the walls to threaten the life of June Allyson.

Allyson has inherited a fortune from her murdered uncle which Angela covets. Aware of the beautiful young heiress' penchant for sleepwalking, Angela lures her toward a nineteenth-floor balcony.

If the whole thing sounds like a silly mishmash of *Gaslight* and *Kind Lady*, it is probably no accident. M-G-M was already well along the path of mediocrity and poor judgment that was to leave it $17.5 million in the red ten years later, and Angela's career was about to hit an all-time low.

41

1952 and 1953 found Angela doing a great deal of television. "Robert Montgomery Presents," "Revlon Mirror Theatre," "Ford Theatre," "Schlitz Playhouse of Stars," "Four Star Playhouse" and "G.E. Theatre" all had the benefit of her talents. Then came three of the worst movies of her career.

The first was *Key Man,* costarring Keith Andes, a film so forgettable no description of it exists in the best anthologies. As for the second, *The Purple Mask,* Angela said, "I was desperate, darling. It was a terrible low point in my career. All I remember is the lunch in the Universal commissary."

The Purple Mask was an unintentional parody of the classic *Scarlet Pimpernel,* with Tony Curtis hopelessly miscast as the French royalist swashbuckler rescuing his fellows from the guillotine during the French Revolution. Angela remembers the guillotine. Critics don't seem to remember her. She plays the seamstress Madame Valentine, fetching enough in period costume, but largely unnoticed. Perhaps it's just as well. What the critics did notice, they laughed at. Bosley Crowther said rather bitingly of Tony Curtis, "He is no Leslie Howard."

Angela may have done *The Purple Mask* because she needed the money, but there was also the lure of a costume piece. The chance to dress in any period other than the twentieth century has always been a temptation for her.

"I have a period face," she says, "which is rather ideal for costume dramas. I always have felt right in costumes, but I do not feel comfortable in modern day dress." James Agee recognized this about Angela and commented on it when he saw her in *Gaslight.*

She would get another chance to dress up as Tally Dickinson, the marshall's girl in *A Lawless Street,* her one and only western, which starred Randolph Scott. It was little compensation for the stereotyped plot and weak-kneed script.

"I once rode off into the sunset on a buckboard with Randolph Scott," she sighs. "Another low point."

Out of costume for the contemporary B-thriller *Please Murder Me,* Angela played the murderess who obligingly kills Raymond Burr.

There was nothing particularly memorable about either the role or the movie. Angela did her usual cool, professional job as yet another bad girl, this time grown up into a full-fledged killer.

Ten television credits later, she was back in costume, this time in a bit of Danny Kaye high camp, *The Court Jester*. Movie-goers had been swamped in recent years by an unprecedented number of knights-in-shining-armor pictures. Sooner or later someone was bound to make fun of these movies. *The Court Jester*, with screenplay by Norman Panama, set to the music of the inimitable Sammy Cahn and the brilliant lyrics of Sylvia Fine (later Mrs. Danny Kaye), did exactly that.

"It stood to reason," Bosley Crowther remarked in a rare display of good humor, "that somebody would eventually cut loose and do a slam-bang burlesque on recent movies about knighthood and der-ring-do. The opportunity was as obvious as the splash of a custard pie. And we are happy to report that it's been leaped at by no less a clown than Danny Kaye, who lands with both feet in *The Court Jester*."

The whimsical tale of a twelfth-century court jester in England who becomes entangled with a desperate band of outlaws attempt-ing to overthrow the king was the perfect vehicle for the irrepressi-ble Kaye, but he also had a lot of help. Though her Princess Gwendolyn is halfway down the list of credits, Angela was not just a fixture. Flirting with Kaye, succumbing to his ardor as the willful princess who dares to love beneath her rank, mooning over him in his absence, trailing around in period costume and stealing scenes simply by being in them, she obviously had a good time after what had been a long run of grim roles. Critics found her performance "dynamic" and "adroit"—welcome words of praise.

The Court Jester is a good swan song for what might be considered the first chapter of her career. Hollywood had underutilized her for too long, and it was time for a change. Her ability to play extremes of youth and age, innocence and evil, subtle tragedy and broad com-edy were always there—her later successes on Broadway prove it—and in the hands of a good director could have been exploited to the fullest. But the fact remains that most times she never got past the casting director. The motion picture industry was and is obsessed with looks, particularly where actresses are concerned; talent is always secondary. Not that Angela didn't keep trying. She went to every casting call she could.

"I was even up for *Forever Amber*," she told Rex Reed during the extraordinary success of *Mame*, when her struggles in the movies seemed very far away. "Whatever would I have used for bosoms?"

That she could keep her sense of humor and bounce back after countless rejections says much about the lady's character. Why Hollywood never truly appreciated her is a mystery buried deep in the recesses of some executive producer's brain. Those who knew film as an art form were more appreciative.

"Not since the heyday of Bette Davis had there been an actress of this range and accomplishment," David Shipman declared in *The Great Movie Stars*. "She was certainly one of the most talented half-dozen women in Hollywood—but after all these years not regarded as a star."

Bette Davis herself paid Angela the compliment of saying matter-of-factly, "You could have played any part I played."

But that praise was to come years later. For now Tinsel Town and Angela Lansbury were about to part company.

"As far as the movies are concerned, I've had it," Angela said at the time. "I've done a lot of puttering around in Hollywood, and the movie people never were really interested in what I could or couldn't do."

She was heading for a new horizon, for a place where after years of hard work she would at last get the recognition she deserved. Hollywood's loss would be Broadway's gain.

> *Broadway has always been a bright light way off in the future, but I finally brought it down to the present . . . I adore comedy. Such a change from the harpies and heavies.*

Angela was to arrive on Broadway after three weeks of breathless rehearsal and an out-of-town run in Washington. The play was *Hotel Paradiso*.

Written in 1886 by the French comedic team of Feydeau and Desvallieres, *Hotel Paradiso* was a bedroom farce in the best of the tradition. It was full of improbable situations revolving around real and imagined infidelities, wives caught between husbands and lovers, and a great deal of door-slamming and running in and out. As translated for a Broadway audience by writer/director Peter Glenville, whose most recent success had been *Separate Tables*, it was the perfect vehicle for one of the greatest clowns of the twentieth century, Bert Lahr.

There is no question that it was Lahr's play. As the philandering husband awaiting the arrival of his best friend's wife, he could say more by just rearranging the creases on his face than most comedians could with pages of dialogue. As theater critic Brooks Atkinson put it, "God must have laughed when he invented Mr. Lahr."

Complementing Mr. Lahr was an energetic and unusual cast. Some were movie actors, and some had a background in revue, mime, or ballet. Others, like Angela, had never done theater on such a level before. But all got caught up in the frenetic ensemble.

"[Mr. Glenville's] actors plunge head-first into a slam-bang performance that goes at high speed, like the silent movies of very many years ago," Atkinson wrote. "The first act arranges the assignation. The second act concludes with a police raid on a disorderly hotel in which . . . the guests are only too well-known to each other. In the third act the authors obligingly solve all the crises and let the audience go happily into the night."

As the wayward wife followed to the hotel by an irate husband, Angela quickly became caught up in the spirit of the play.

"It's the kind of acting I've never done before," she told *Herald Tribune* reporter Helen Ormsbee. "Comedy at a fast pace, with all of us opening and shutting doors, and running up and down stairs, in Paris in 1910. At first one of our problems was how to rush around like that and have breath enough to say our lines. But we're used to it now. There are so many quick twists of the plot that we couldn't begin to act our parts till we knew everyone's lines and actions so well that things fell into a rhythm. That is how we do it now, so it's great fun."

The great fun began with a call from director Glenville, a close friend of Peter's. He wanted Angela and no one else for the role of Marcelle, offering it to her, in Angela's words, "on a platter."

"I was steeped in domesticity when Peter called me," Angela remembers. "I hopped on a plane and with only three weeks of rehearsals opened in Washington. When we came to Broadway I was scared spitless."

Settling into a brownstone in Manhattan's east fifties, she immediately sent for the children, their governess Miss Fyffe, "and my best teapot. It took one heck of a push to persuade myself to leave my family and our home in California. I never dreamed [the play] would catch on like this. This is a real fling for Mum."

The play did catch on, and so did Angela. Reviews cited her "fine sense of humor." Brooks Atkinson found her "wildly funny" as "a high-strung wife who is forever throwing her arms in the air." And *New York Post* staff writer Kevin Delaney, in an observation little short of prophecy, said, "She has a classic chin-high manner which has theater written all over it."

Angela, perhaps a little overwhelmed by the sudden critical praise, still managed to keep things in perspective.

46

"I was awed and thrilled even to be asked," she says of the *Hotel Paradiso* experience. "Because I always considered appearing in the theater a rung higher than acting in movies. Because, obviously, one had to be more accomplished to act on stage than on film."

The awe was balanced by the fun, and the glamor of dressing up in the extravagant costumes topped with a heavy blonde Gibson girl wig.

"Can you imagine that topped off with the wide straw hat heavy with roses that I wear in the second act, and summer's searing temperatures?" she asked of one interviewer, her ability to poke fun at herself showing through.

In contrast to her stage personality, the offstage Angela tended not to dress up unless she absolutely had to, confining her wardrobe to a couple of suits, the really dressy dresses one wore to Hollywood premieres, and lots of sweaters and slacks. The "look" in New York that season tended toward proper little dresses and heels; it was unheard of to go anywhere without white gloves and the right hat. Asked how she dealt with fashion's dictates, the independent Angela shrugged, "I generally solve the problem by not going out before five. After that, evening clothes are acceptable."

But for all her sophistication, there is still a trace of the wide-eyed teen-ager caught rubbernecking at the Broadway marquees just after the war.

"I felt completely lost in the city," she admits. "Happy to find refuge in my dressing room every evening."

She compensated for the loneliness by being with Anthony and Deirdre as much as possible with eight performances a week. The apartment was cluttered with Deirdre's dollhouse and Anthony's crayons, the walls plastered with his drawings of "animuls."

Miss Fyffe brought the children to the theater between shows on matinee days. Angela would show them around backstage, anxious to make them understand why "Mum" had to disappear every night, to answer their endless "whys" about where she worked and what she did with her life. Between shows she and the children would have dinner in a favorite restaurant before Angela went on for the evening's performance.

47

Sometimes her eagerness to have her children share in her life backfired, producing particularly painful scenes. "They saw part of a matinee one day," Angela reminisced, "but when John Emery, playing my husband in the show, got angry with me, Anthony couldn't bear it." Anthony was only five. His mother's acting must have been extremely believable to him. "He cried. He didn't want that man to be cross with me, he said. I explained to him that in a play people are only pretending."

Already Anthony was showing the sensitivity so often the heritage of children of creative parents. Angela, who had already been rehearsing her cabaret act when she was not much older than her own children at this time, wondered if either of them would have a theatrical bent. Would it have been better to leave her children behind in Hollywood with their father, to keep her career a secret from them? Angela remained adamant that she had chosen the best way.

"Whatever I'm engaged in, or my husband is working at, our family won't be separated for any length of time," she declared. "No matter where we are, we'll make a home."

When *Hotel Paradiso* closed after a healthy six-month run, home became Hollywood once again.

The Long, Hot Summer was part of the wait. Derived from several short stories by William Faulkner, with a touch of Tennessee Williams' *Cat On A Hot Tin Roof,* the film was a tautly written bit of cinematic realism. It had the advantage of a skilled, highly believable cast, which included Paul Newman, Joanne Woodward, Orson Welles, Lee Remick, and Angela.

In the small southern town of Frenchman's Bend, a young roughneck (Paul Newman) with a suspicious past, worms his way into the favor of the local rich man (Orson Welles), systematically casting suspicion on the old man's heirs so that he can inherit the estate. One of his targets is Minnie, the rich man's mistress.

Admittedly the part of Minnie was a showy role, written with a degree of depth. Minnie is kindhearted, warm, and although definite in her plans to marry Varner, the audience becomes convinced it is more for love than money. Critics were impressed with the film.

"The whole show," Bosley Crowther wrote, "has the look and the atmospheric feeling of an afternoon storm making up above the still trees and sun-cracked buildings of a quiet southern town on a hot day."

At least part of that look and feeling had to do with the supporting cast, including a young Lee Remick (with whom Angela was to work again on several occasions) as the not-too-bright daughter-in-law, and Angela. Crowther, however, paid Angela what can only be considered a backhanded compliment, "Angela Lansbury makes a good fleshy old doll," he wrote.

Angela was just past thirty. Was Crowther implying that he had been so caught up by her performance that he forgot how young she was? One might stretch a point in trying to believe that, but the remark must have stung.

"Hollywood made me old before my time," Angela would quip in an interview years later, referring to all those roles in which she'd had to be made up to add years or sometimes decades to her age.

When she was barely into her twenties, she frequently got fan mail from people who thought she was in her forties. As late as 1979 when she did *The Mirror Crack'd,* she was still being hidden behind a white wig and age lines to play Miss Marple. Even today, on the set of "Murder, She Wrote," a crew member can be overheard to remark "It's hard to believe she's over seventy-five!"

"It happens all the time," Angela smiles. "I'm surprised a lot of people don't think I'm eighty-five!"

She can laugh about it now, but when she was only in her thirties it must have hurt.

Her next film not only would age her, it would begin the string of "mother" roles that long characterized her movie career. The contrast between *The Long, Hot Summer* and *The Reluctant Debutante* couldn't have been more extreme. Critic A.H. Weiler described the latter as "a fragile thing made bright and gay by uninhibited principles and some of the season's frothiest dialogue. The resulting *Reluctant Debutante* is thin and boneless but nonetheless giddy and diverting."

As the title suggests, the picture was about the coming out of a young society deb (Sandra Dee) and her unwillingness to be put "on the block" and auctioned off to the most suitable marriage partner. The film's entire flimsy plot deals with the rivalries of wealthy parents trying to matchmake for their daughters.

It is the parents who steal this film from the young people who are supposed to win the audience's sympathy. Rex Harrison and the late Kay Kendall (at that time also married in real life) as Sandra

Dee's parents were in direct competition with Angela, as the mother of another deb.

The cattiness and flippant rivalry between these two otherwise best friends and confidantes is captivating and entertaining. It is made especially poignant in retrospect because this was to be the last film Kay Kendall ever made. She had been diagnosed with myeloid leukemia over a year before and given less than two years to live. Worse, she didn't even know. Rex Harrison, who had ended his long marriage to Lilli Palmer solely to be with Kay (he'd had the nerve to ask Lilli if he could come back to her "when it was all over"), had lacked the courage to tell her the truth. Somehow everyone else on the set seemed to know.

"It was so sad because we all knew Kay was dying," Angela remembers. "It was a terrible time for Rex."

In addition to having to keep the traditional British stiff upper lip because of Kay's health, Harrison was beset with tax problems that necessitated shooting this very British film at a studio in Paris. If nothing else, *The Reluctant Debutante* gave Angela a chance to travel.

Her next film was to take her further afield. Burdened with the awkward title of *Summer Of The Seventeenth Doll* (it was released in Britain as *Season Of Passion*), this rather trashy story of a pair of tarts who entertain a new set of men every summer suffered from a number of other liabilities as well.

Based on an Australian play, it fell prey to mixed casting from both England and America and not one of the many accomplished performers managed to find and maintain a recognizable Aussie accent. Anne Baxter, John Mills, and Ernest Borgnine floundered along with Angela in a movie that might have been better off never being made. Possibly its producers thought so as well. United Artists didn't release *Seventeenth Doll* until 1961, more than two years after it was made.

One of the brighter spots in that period was a chance to do two episodes of "Playhouse 90," among the best of the television anthologies, and one for which Angela's baby brother Edgar was now a producer.

Both Bruce and Edgar had become highly successful in television. Bruce remained on the west coast, as writer/producer for KABC Television. He would later join CBS, becoming producer of such shows as "Wild, Wild West" and "Mission, Impossible."

Edgar, after attending U.C.L.A. with his twin brother, studied design at the Otis Art Institute in Los Angeles, and apprenticed as scenic designer and art director at the Windham Playhouse in New Hampshire. He had done scenic design for "The Red Skelton Show" and "Studio One" as well as "Playhouse 90," before becoming producer. None of the Lansburys were going to let the grass grow under their feet.

Meanwhile, Angela got a chance at a sympathetic role for a change, as what she always referred to as "that heartbreaking woman"—Mavis in *The Dark At The Top Of The Stairs.*

Adapted from William Inge's stage play of the same name, the film dealt with what one critic called "the tensions and the heartaches of an average family." Robert Preston is the husband/father/harness salesman hero who has recently lost his job. Dorothy McGuire is his frigid, nagging wife. In the stage version the frustrated husband sought comfort in the arms of a well-meaning widow who never appeared onstage. In the movie version, the role was written in for Angela.

Her Mavis is soft and comforting, a self-supporting beauty salon proprietress who makes up in empathy what she may lack in sophistication. And while she may suffer the salesman's desperate embraces, she never lets him go too far, and ultimately sends him back to his wife.

In an attempt to appeal to a wider audience than the play received, the film may have gone overboard, taking what could have been tender moments and turning them mawkish. Few movie-goers appreciate how a poor script can frustrate even the best actors. It is embarrassing to see performers of the calibre of Preston, McGuire, Eve Arden, and Angela struggle against sloppy dialogue, glaring camera techniques, and a hokey musical score. Angela poured her heart into this role, only to earn mixed reviews.

"Angela Lansbury makes a prepossessing widow who is just too noble for anybody's good," was the general assessment of the critical community.

Proving that it was possible to go from a good role in a bad movie to a bad role in a worse movie, Angela next found herself in Vienna for *A Breath Of Scandal*. This silly adaptation of a dated Ferenc Molnar play, about a Hapsburg princess whose reputation is ruined by spending an innocent night in a hunting lodge with a handsome American, was a horrific waste of talent and money. Sophia Loren, John Gavin, Maurice Chevalier, Isabel Jeans, Angela, and a European supporting cast promenaded about the rococo palaces of Vienna in feathered hats and paste jewels, spreading malicious gossip and whispering knowingly about the emperor.

Angela got a chance to sink her claws into yet another nasty character, the malicious Princess Lina of Ruritania, who tries to destroy Sophia Loren with her vicious insinuation. The opportunity to see Vienna and play another costume role might have been fun, but it hardly helped her break the stranglehold of typecasting.

No doubt Angela recognized this, but she did her professional best to put a brave face on it. She was characteristically gracious about her fellow actors and their director, Michael Curtiz. When the Italian Loren encountered difficulties with the language barrier, Angela remembers, "Sophia didn't understand a word Mike said, and yet he was a very good director."

Of her own performance in *Breath Of Scandal* and most of the other films of that period, she can only say, "I am sometimes put off by a character I abhor, a person I would not want to be with in real life. I've played so many dreadful women. You can't keep on doing those roles."

Anyone else might have given up, stayed home and watched her children grow, and tended her Tropicana roses.

"All those years I had this vision that someday I'd blossom forth, that I'd show everybody what I was really capable of. I could see myself singing, dancing, carrying on, being the life of the party, hogging the limelight—the works. Nobody knew, not even my family. But I knew."

The opportunity to do all these things was in the cards, but not yet. Angela was about to be lured back to Broadway, by no less a light than David Merrick. But singing and dancing were not what he had in mind. *A Taste Of Honey* was a provocative and controversial play about a lonely white girl who has an affair with a black sailor and chooses to have his baby—volatile subject matter in the racially troubled early sixties. Playwright Shelagh Delaney was only nineteen when she wrote her troubling work. The setting in her native Lancashire, and the way in which she explores the desolation and loneliness of her characters' lives, suggests that much of her material may have been at least partly autobiographical.

"Miss Delaney's play does not seem to be constructed. It unfolds with the naturalness and apparent irrelevancy of daily living," was how one critic described it.

The young and gifted British actress Joan Plowright was cast as the girl, Josephine. Years later she was to become Mrs. Laurence Olivier. By wonderful coincidence, her future husband opened on Broadway in Anouilh's *Becket* in the same week, only two blocks away from *A Taste Of Honey*. The sailor, known in the play only as "The Boy," was to be played by a very young but no less handsome Billy Dee Williams. Veteran English actor Nigel Davenport and a sensitive Andrew Ray made up the rest of this small, intimate cast.

The role of Josephine's mother required a special kind of actress. On first glance this was another thankless role, another mother role, but given the Lansbury touch it was to become much more. Producer David Merrick sent Angela a copy of the script, and in a series of long distance calls from New York, proceeded to win her over.

"Helen was a provocative, fascinating part," Angela remembers. "I didn't want to leave my family and go to New York, but I couldn't resist the part."

When it was obvious that the play would enjoy a long run, Angela was to solve the problem by bringing her family to New York with her. Anthony and Deirdre, who were now aged nine and eight, shared her Manhattan apartment. A private tutor was engaged to help them keep up with their schoolwork. Husband Peter flew in from the coast whenever his schedule with William Morris permitted. Christmas dinner that year found them all together at a cosy little family restaurant that Angela remembers as "very *gemüt-lichkeit*." As Angela had promised herself back during the run of *Hotel Paradiso,* she and Peter would make a home wherever they were.

The critics found *A Taste Of Honey* fascinating, if gritty and somewhat disheartening. "It is not a pretty story," *New York Times* drama critic Howard Taubman wrote. "It is not even tragic because its characters make no effort to defy their fates. But it is filled with wry laughter, and it is all the more moving because it does not tear the emotions to tatters."

The ability to create that kind of delicate, fine-tuned characterization, and to sustain it for *Honey*'s six-month run, was both challenging and exhausting. Angela gave it her best—it was so refreshing to at last have a role that gave her a chance to stretch—but found the experience was harrowing.

"I was playing a very sad woman, and I had to rev myself up every night," she says, remembering it. "It was getting to me. It shouldn't have, but it was."

Whatever the personal cost, she had achieved a level of performance to which both audiences and critics responded.

"Angela Lansbury plays the mother with quicksilver that does not conceal the seaminess of her life," Taubman wrote, citing the "cheerful and brittle indifference" of this "raffish mother, a woman who has gamy tastes" in her choices of men, "picking up yet another man in a life full of all sorts."

It is the sad, bitter tawdriness of her boozy, utterly selfish mother that makes Josephine's one brief interlude of love so poignant by contrast. Much of the success of *A Taste Of Honey* is due to the dynamism between the two characters. It is a generous actress who can risk making her character look bad in order to make a play work. Angela is such an actress. Joan Plowright may have won a Tony for her performance, but it is safe to say that she got a lot of help from Angela. Still, the play took its toll, and Angela was rather relieved when it was over.

"I wanted to wash my hands of it and get back to the sunshine of my own life," she says in retrospect.

*O*ne of Angela's remarkable gifts is the ability to look at and judge herself objectively. Some of this may be the result of her theater training; the rest is purely strength of character.

"I never thought I was pretty," she says of her youth. "I was always self-conscious. I had a very beautiful mother. Maybe the psychologists would say that's why I felt that way about myself."

Time and maturity would ultimately change her opinion, make her more secure with herself. "I've grown into myself," she can say now. "In the past I always felt I had to look like someone else. Now I can look like myself."

She can even be objective about one of the grimmest phases of her life.

"When I was about thirty-five, I started dressing as though I was fifty-five. Suddenly I became very settled—broad in the beam. When I did *Manchurian Candidate* I was very fat, and quite middle-aged looking. I think I was probably willing myself to be middle-aged."

In an industry where looks are everything, it seems almost suicidal for an actress to let herself go this way. But Angela was still determined to prove that she could make it on talent alone.

Her refusal to be like other actresses in Hollywood got her roles that can only qualify, in her own words, as "a series of stinkers." One of the worst of these had to be as Elvis Presley's mother in *Blue*

Hawaii. It was such a stinker even Dolores del Rio, an actress hardly in Angela's league, turned it down.

"That was the lowest, darling, I was desperate," Angela was to tell *Los Angeles Times* columnist Robert Windeler.

Another actress might have phoned in a half-hearted performance, taken the money and run. But Angela isn't made that way. She managed to give Sarah Lee Gates sufficient dottiness and appeal to upstage even "The King."

No one has ever suffered from the delusion that an Elvis Presley movie was anything more than an excuse to display its star on the big screen, and let him croon and gyrate his way through a dozen or so songs loosely strung together against an exotic background. In *Blue Hawaii* the plot has Elvis as an ex-GI returning to his family's pineapple plantation, deciding this is not the life for him, and running off to frolic on the beach with a handful of bongo-playing pals and one very cute island girl.

Mama and Papa are furious with young Chad, of course. They want him to be respectable and marry a girl from the proper social class. Through a series of misadventures, all set to music, Mama and Papa come to see the light, Elvis gets the girl, and everyone goes off singing into the Technicolor sunset.

In the few scenes of this foolishness she is allowed to appear in, Angela is a wonderful latter day Scarlett O'Hara gone hopelessly to seed on her pineapple plantation. She constantly misunderstands everything everybody says, and her grasp on reality is tenuous. When for about the fifth time she mentions "her Chadwick's being home from the war," Roland Winters, as her stuffy, long-suffering husband, loses his temper, shouting at her that there *wasn't* any war.

"Well, if I don't keep telling myself there was a war, I just have to believe Chadwick wasted two years of his life," is Sarah Lee's perfectly logical retort.

Finishing *Blue Hawaii,* Angela found yet another mother role awaiting her, though both mother and son were quite different from those in the piece of fluff she'd just finished.

The early sixties was the era of "momism," American pop psychology's attempt to blame everyone's neuroses on their mothers.

James Leo Herlihy's novel *All Fall Down* was about momism at its worst. And William Inge's script for the movie version made both mom and her elder son among the most loathsome creatures ever to inhabit the silver screen.

As played by Warren Beatty, the son is a surly, brutish, overgrown spoiled brat. For some reason his entire family and half the women in his hometown of Cleveland adore him. He drives one woman to suicide, drives his family to distraction, and when getting drunk doesn't help alleviate his malaise, he packs up and leaves for Florida.

Critics took director John Frankenheimer to task for "encouraging Mr. Beatty to develop an image that would be as individual as that of the young Marlon Brando or the late James Dean." They found nothing redeemable about either the character of the son or the movie in general. The young man's parents, however, garnered mixed reviews.

"Certainly the mother and father are a little mad," Bosley Crowther wrote. "The mother, whom Angela Lansbury makes a most rash, possessive 'mom,' comes close to being psychopathic in her attentiveness to her older son. And the father, played by Karl Malden with a beady, wild look in his eye, is nutty as well as alcoholic. It is possible to believe in them. It is also possible to imagine that exposure to them might drive a sensitive son away from home."

David Shipman found it easy to blame the young man's troubles on Angela's mom. "She is an irritating, possessive mother with shades of incest, whose nonstop chattering and bossiness drove Warren Beatty to drink, distraction, and other problems." By contrast, critic Pauline Kael found her "at times extraordinarily moving, reminiscent of Bette Davis at her best."

Angela managed to create a monstrous mother for the screen. Director Frankenheimer was to recognize that monstrousness, and use it again most effectively in *The Manchurian Candidate*.

"From the artistic point of view I love these parts," Angela says. "You see, I lack guts in my own life. I lack fire and meanness—so I love playing it in screen roles. I am rather a sensitive person, and I think you have to be a sensitive person to play it nasty.

"It isn't true that you have to be one to play one," she adds mischievously. "I have seen real bitches in Hollywood play soft sentimental roles so beautifully I wept."

At about the time that *All Fall Down* was being shot, Vincente Minnelli was directing a remake of *The Four Horsemen Of The Apocalypse.* The 1921 Rex Ingram version of Ibanez's epic novel about love and death in the First World War had been a star vehicle for Rudolph Valentino. M-G-M's 1962 remake starred Glenn Ford in the Valentino role, and other roles were equally miscast. Ingrid Thulin, Paul Henreid, Charles Boyer, Paul Lukas, Yvette Mimieux, Karl Boehm and Lee J. Cobb were largely wasted in the film and, according to John Douglas Eames in *The M-G-M Story:*

". . . Minnelli's sensitivity was out to lunch. The dialogue in the Robert Ardrey-John Gay script was so banal, and the depiction of wartime Paris in Julian Blaustein's production so faulty, that giggles punctuated its press screenings."

To make matters worse, an already in the red Metro lost six million dollars on the debacle. The film is mentioned here for one reason. Though she is not listed in the credits, Angela was involved in *Four Horsemen Of The Apocalypse,* or at least her voice was. Metro executives were so dissatisfied with Ingrid Thulin's line readings that all her dialogue was redubbed by Angela. Why Vincente Minnelli, whose sensitivity in directing women was almost equal to George Cukor's, couldn't have cast Angela in the role from the beginning is a mystery. But considering the outcome, he may have done her a favor.

Of all the moms Angela was to play in the sixties, none was so perfectly evil, so bone chillingly sinister as Mrs. Iselin in *The Manchurian Candidate.*

The premise of the film, based on Richard Condon's novel about an American POW released from a North Korean prison camp after being "programmed" to assassinate a presidential candidate, terrified countless movie-goers in that post-McCarthy era. Movie critics were less easily frightened.

"This story of a moody young fellow who was captured by the

Communists during the Korean campaign and brainwashed by them to do their bidding as a high-level assassin when he gets home to America is as wild a piece of fiction as anything Alfred Hitchcock might present," Bosley Crowther remarked drily.

In truth the critics were not sure what to make of this film, which was in some respects ahead of its time. Directed by John Frankenheimer, known for his handling of dark material, backed in part by political right-winger Frank Sinatra (who also stars in the movie), *The Manchurian Candidate* is on one level a warning about the menace of the "yellow peril"—communist China. On another level, however, it can be viewed as a warning about mind control in any form. Whether the intensive programming to which young Raymond (Laurence Harvey) is subjected in the prison camp, or the red-baiting media hype his senator/stepfather (James Gregory) practices in front of American news cameras, brainwashing is an evil in anybody's hands.

The film was a trailblazer in that it assumed an intelligent and receptive audience. Hollywood had long thought of its audience as children easily entertained by formulaic films. Frankenheimer took a risk with *Manchurian Candidate,* and to a large extent the risk paid off. More than twenty years later the film is still valid as art, even if its premise seems a little dated and hysterical.

Manchurian Candidate would have its audience believe that not only has Raymond been brainwashed by the Chinese (and in only three days), but his mother, on the surface as right-wing as her husband, is in fact a communist operative who is part of the assassination plot. It is she who "triggers" the patterns implanted in Raymond's brain, forcing him to do the bidding of his "masters" behind the "bamboo curtain."

As written, the character of Raymond's mother may have stretched the bounds of credibility, but Angela's meticulous, relentless portrayal was right on target. Bosley Crowther called her "intense"; David Shipman found her "impervious and chilling as Mrs. Iselin." She is so unnatural as a mother that she makes Lady Macbeth look like the president of the PTA. And in true "justice and the American way" fashion, she gets blown away at the end.

The film *is* incredibly violent, working its way up from karate fights that leave whole rooms in shambles to Raymond's cold-blooded elimination of a liberal senator and the senator's daughter, whom he once loved, to the climactic assassination scene at a presidential convention in Madison Square Garden, complete with hundreds of extras dressed in Abe Lincoln costumes.

Raymond also murders his manipulative mother. When young Anthony Shaw was asked what part of the film he'd liked best, he turned toward his mother, and with an eleven-year-old's chilling candor said, "The part where you get shot right between the eyes."

The remark may have been innocent, just a little boy showing off for an interviewer. But it also suggests that Anthony might have been less than comfortable with his mother's profession.

"My little boy wants me to take off my makeup as soon as I come in from the studio," Angela admitted at the time. She was well aware of Anthony's sensitivity, but there didn't seem to be much she could do about it.

Deirdre, on the other hand, seemed untroubled by her mother's many faces. At ten the young lady had been studying piano for several years, and already knew what she wanted to be when she grew up—a jazz pianist. Angela's influence can be seen in her daughter's creative bent; she had always hoped both her children would do "something creative."

"I tell them that they do not, and should not, have to conform to the dictates of a group," she declared adamantly. At the same time, neither she nor Peter ever coddled their children or tried to protect them from life. "Children should have disappointments. It is the sweetest thing in the world to see a child get over a disappointment."

The contrast between the real-life Angela and the evil mothers she played onscreen could not be more evident. Add to this the fact that she was only three years older than her "son" Laurence Harvey in *The Manchurian Candidate,* and it is clear just how good an actress she is. One story has it that President John F. Kennedy, who had read the Richard Condon novel, was extremely interested in the making of *The Manchurian Candidate.* Hobnobbing with Frank Sinatra, perennial friend of presidents, Kennedy inquired about casting. When told Angela Lansbury would be playing Raymond's mother, he was reported to be "highly pleased."

The Manchurian Candidate turned out to be one of the president's favorite films. Considering that it opened less than thirteen months before his assassination by an unlikely candidate not too very different from Raymond Shaw, its prophetic message may not have been so hysterical after all.

*N*ext to "mom," evil or otherwise, the second most common type-casting for a middle-aged actress has always been the cold, insensitive, emasculating wife. Angela played her share of those, too.

In The Cool Of The Day was a big-screen soap opera, complete with exotic locations in London and Greece and a stellar cast which, given something resembling a decent script, could have made a decent movie. Instead, actors of the calibre of Peter Finch, Arthur Hill, Constance Cummings, and relative newcomer Jane Fonda struggled with performances that ranged from nervous jitters to obvious boredom.

Peter Finch is a British publisher unhappily married to carping, discontented Angela. Jane Fonda is a latter day Camille, suffering from some unspecified malady, caught between her overly solicitous husband (Arthur Hill) and her nagging mother (Constance Cummings). Publisher and invalid fall in love against the backdrop of the Acropolis. Perhaps the Greek ruins were intended as a metaphor for the wreck of their respective marriages. At any rate, the beautiful invalid dies, and so does the movie.

Angela's place in this muddle was somewhere between Peter Finch's "peculiarly listless performance," as movie critic Howard Thompson described it, and Jane Fonda's jitters. She gives a cool performance as the wife, surly and spiteful enough to drive any man into another woman's arms, while gliding about in classy designer costumes through the glamorous habitats of publishing's upper echelons. But she may have made a common mistake. Too many actors read a script only for *their* part, not taking into consideration that the script as a whole may be so weak even the most dazzling performance can't save it. This would seem to be the shortcoming of *In The Cool Of The Day*. Otherwise it was a harmless bit of escapism, a chance to travel the continent without ever leaving the movie theater, and a glimpse of the loneliness "at the top," always a sure-fire draw in middle America.

It is almost impossible to find an actor working in the mid-sixties who was *not* in *The Greatest Story Ever Told*. If a single movie could epitomize the American film industry's philosophy of "more is better," this was it.

Completed on a *five-year* production schedule, its premiere running time was a whopping four hours and twenty minutes. Subsequent cuts reduced it to 238 minutes. It was shown in Britain at 197 minutes and, finally, in America at 190 minutes, usually in two parts with an intermission. But it is still overlong and, finally, pointless. According to *The Video Sourcebook,* the entire epic can be summed up in a single sentence: "Christ's journey from Galilee to Golgotha and the world of saints, sinners and believers that appear along the way."

Shot between October, 1962 and July, 1963, the film was not released until 1965. *The Bible On Film: A Checklist, 1897-1980* states, "It tried too hard to be the ultimate in religious films and in doing so, failed miserably. It was too long, there was stilted and some unintentionally amusing dialogue, and the film was overly dominated by cameo appearances by name stars. It did not do too well at the box office."

This despite producer/director George Stevens' optimistic claim at the start that it "would still be showing at the end of the century and after." Stevens also earned the film its first bad publicity, and some of its bigger chuckles, by telling reporters he would not be shooting on location in Palestine as had originally been planned, but in the desert in Utah, because "Utah looks more like Palestine."

With a blond, blue-eyed Max von Sydow as Jesus, Dorothy McGuire as Mary, and Pat Boone as the Angel at the Tomb, over sixty featured players, the Inbal Dance Theatre of Israel, and a few thousand extras, the film didn't seem to be able to do anything right. It has the distinction of earning *The Harvard Lampoon's* Worst Film Award for 1965, in the company of such screen gems as *Station Six Sahara* and *Kiss Me, Stupid*.

As one of the dozens of featured players, Angela appears briefly as the Roman matron Claudia, seen flirting with Telly Savalas' Pontius Pilate. As a reporter from *Variety* quipped, Angela was "only a flash in the Panavision."

The World Of Henry Orient put her back in the straitjacket, albeit a luxurious one, as the mink-clad momma of an upper east side Manhattan urchin (Tippy Walker) who has a crush on an offbeat concert pianist (Peter Sellers). The film was as offbeat as its title character, who is as affected and snobbish, as flaky and lecherous as only Peter Sellers could be. The two moonstruck teens who follow him to chic restaurants and spy on him as he carries on an affair with another man's wife provide an interesting perspective on the hypocrisy of the adult world in general.

Angela and Tom Bosley, as the parents of one of these poor little rich girls, provide further examples of that hypocrisy. Caught up in their own lives, they all but abandon their daughter, practically allowing her to live on the streets. For once Angela plays a "mean mother" of a different ilk. Rather than the possessive/obsessive mother of a brutish son, she is the distant/indifferent mother of a waiflike daughter. She even flirts with Henry Orient herself, oblivious to her daughter's needs. Critics gave her and Bosley high scores for the realism of their performances.

Henry Orient was a message film, artfully conceived and executed. Considering some of the stinkers she'd had to work in before, it must have been rewarding to work in a film worthy of Angela's complete dedication. It is an example of the old saying that there are no small parts, only small actors.

Angela had one more stinker role before her career suddenly changed directions. *Dear Heart,* described by its producers as a "gay, sophisticated comedy," was in film critic Bosley Crowther's opinion just the opposite. He called it "a stale, dull and humorless pretension" that "makes almost scandalous misuse of the recognized talents of Geraldine Page."

Miss Page plays a spinsterish small-town postmistress who has a tawdry affair with a traveling greeting card salesman (Glenn Ford). The simplistic plot is mildly complicated by the salesman's lady friend back home, a plumpish widow with an obnoxious young son, who is about to interrupt the sad little romance. The widow/mother, of course, is played by Angela Lansbury.

Crowther spends most of his very short review lamenting the fate of Geraldine Page. That *Dear Heart* by and large misused the talents of all its actors didn't seem to bother him too much. After some insulting remarks about Glenn Ford, he dismisses the rest of the cast as "equally charmless," including in his blanket condemnation Angela's portrayal of the "bumptious mother."

Blaming the failure of a performance piece solely on its actors is a cheap shot. It's especially hard to take from a critic, who ought to be well versed in the ensemble of a film or play, the combination of script, director, actors, technicians, set and wardrobe designers, etc. necessary to create the whole. But as Angela was about to discover, it was harder still to take this attitude from the very producers of the show one is putting one's heart into.

Everybody says "don't"
Everybody says "can't"
Everybody says wait around for miracles
That's the way the world is made . . .
I say "don't"
Don't be afraid!

—*"EVERYBODY SAYS DON'T"*
FROM *Anyone Can Whistle*

Only one thing is harder to predict than the weather—the success or failure of a Broadway musical. Take a book by Arthur Laurents, whose previous credits included *Home Of The Brave, Time Of The Cuckoo, West Side Story* and *Gypsy,* mix well with music and lyrics by Broadway's boy wonder Stephen Sondheim, who had worked with Laurents on *West Side Story* and *Gypsy,* add a fresh, energetic cast, stir well, and you have a sure-fire recipe, right? Not necessarily.

Anyone Can Whistle had all of these ingredients, besides being fresh. The musical numbers were bubbly and daring, similar in flavor to *The Fantasticks,* which had been bouncing merrily along off-Broadway for nearly four years. Most of all, *Anyone Can Whistle* was different. Too different. That was why, after a troubled out-of-town run, it braved Broadway for nine performances, and folded.

Laurents, Sondheim, et al. forgot one thing. People who pay Broadway prices for Broadway musicals don't want different. They want more of the same. The Laurents/Sondheim combination had dared to be different with *West Side Story* six years earlier. After a shaky beginning the show held on, took on, and took off. Today it is

67

considered a classic. *Anyone Can Whistle* might have done the same. Maybe.

The show's problem was its premise—a tongue-in-cheek proposition that conformity equals insanity and only the "nuts" of this world are sane. Broadway audiences failed to see the humor in this idea. And to take this notion seriously frightened them. If *Anyone Can Whistle* had opened in 1968 or 69 instead of 1964, it might have been a smash.

In his book *Broadway Musicals,* drama critic Martin Gottfried describes *Anyone Can Whistle* as "a cult show, the sort that would have run forever if everyone who claims to have seen it actually bought tickets."

And indeed, those who *did* see it loved it. There just weren't enough of them. And the show's one-week run didn't leave time for word-of-mouth to bring it a larger audience.

Angela remembers, "When I did *Anyone Can Whistle*—a magnificent failure—the crowd yelled bravo. But that was the insypoo New York crowd. They're marvelous, but they fizzle out in six weeks."

Angela's involvement in *Whistle* began with, of all things, a personal inquiry from writer Arthur Laurents.

"Dear Miss Lansbury," he wrote to her in 1963. "I am writing a musical play. Have you ever sung? Would you be interested in appearing in a musical? Would you consider my sending you a script?"

The tone of the letter was positively deferential. Laurents was not only offering her a part, he was implying he might actually be writing it with her in mind. It had been a long time since anyone had tailored a role specifically for Angela's talents—as long ago as *Dorian Gray.* And no one had ever offered her a chance to carry an original role in a Broadway musical. This was the actress who had had her voice dubbed over in recordings of *The Harvey Girls* because producers didn't think it was strong enough. The invitation was exhilarating and impossible to resist.

"I always fancied I had a sexy singing voice but no one would ever let me use it," Angela says. "When *Whistle* was offered to me I grabbed it."

Her reply to Laurents' asking her if she would care to read

the script? "Would I? Send it to me. I'm yours."

Angela read the play, which took place in a small industrial town. When the only factory shuts down, the citizens manufacture a fake "miracle" in order to drum up a tourist trade. The miracle consists of a spring with supposedly curative powers flowing from a rock in the center of town. All goes well until the local mental institution, called The Cookie Jar, sends its patients to the rock for a cure. The miracle is finally exposed as a hoax, but not before the "cookies'" dedicated nurse (Lee Remick) and the town's even more dedicated doctor (Harry Guardino) fall in love, and it is suggested that normal people, hidebound and conventional, could stand to learn a few things from the cookies. "I wasn't sure I understood it," Angela admits. "But I knew it was brilliant."

The part Laurents wanted Angela to play was that of the town's swinging gutsy mayoress. How could the daughter and grand-daughter of the politically active Lansburys and ex-mayoress Moyna MacGill possibly refuse?

She hadn't had a chance to sing professionally since *Dorian Gray.* But the gutsiness that had her singing to cabaret audiences while still in her teens pulled her through the audition.

"I had a tiny bit of vocal coaching, and then I sang 'A Foggy Day in London Town' for Arthur and Stephen Sondheim," Angela remembers, adding with her characteristic ability to poke fun at herself, "It wasn't terribly good but it was loud—so they seemed optimistic and signed me."

If it occurred to her that she was going out on a limb, taking a big chance, Angela didn't let it bother her. For one thing she had Laurents and Sondheim in her corner. For another, she has always known what she could do, given half a chance. She was about to take to heart some lines from "Everybody Says Don't," one of *Whistle's* songs:

> Sometimes you have to start slow
> Climbing the tiniest wall
> Maybe you're going to fall
> But it's better than not starting at all.

She was even willing, as the song suggests in a later verse, to:

Fall if you have to
But, lady, make a noise.

The lady was about to make a noise, possibly not as big as she'd hoped, but a noise that would have later repercussions. The first thing she did was to begin a crash diet and get herself back into shape. No more middle-aged blues for this lady.

"[*Whistle*] was a real second wind for me, because it was my emergence into the musical environment, a whole set of new things, and it broadened me enormously, as a performer and as a person, too. It really changed my life a lot."

While she may have been puzzled by Arthur Laurents' book for *Anyone Can Whistle*—a puzzlement later to be shared by drama critics—she had absolute faith in Stephen Sondheim's words and music. "Do you know I really believe that the score is the best Steve Sondheim has ever written?" she says, though she has done *Gypsy* and *Sweeney Todd* since. "It was so melodic and brilliant and clever."

Former *New York Post* theater critic Martin Gottfried shares Angela's enthusiasm. "Sondheim's music and lyrics, like the youthful work of Porter and Coward, burst with spirit and wit. The whole radiated more sheer energy than any subseqent work of his. It is also the most 'Broadway' of his scores, spirited and brassy . . . The score contained long sequences of interwoven story, music and dance that foreshadowed the Sondheim to come. There was no way of telling where Laurents' book left off and Sondheim's lyrics began, or when Herbert Ross's wonderful dances were becoming Laurents' direction."

At thirty-four, Stephen Sondheim was still considered Broadway's wunderkind. He had been only twenty-seven when his lyrics for *West Side Story* offered audiences his very distinctive voice. He had blockbusters like *Gypsy* and *A Funny Thing Happened On The Way To The Forum* behind him, and *Sweeney Todd* and *Pacific Overtures* still to come. The boy who at fifteen had shown Oscar Hammerstein II the score for a school play he had written, then stood still while the Broadway veteran tore it to shreds—constructively—apparently could do no wrong.

"This is music for the musical comedy stage, informed by a classical background," Martin Gottfried concludes.

The show's conductor, Herbert Greene, however, was less than impressed. Handed Sondheim's score, as orchestrated by Don Walker, he saw nothing but trouble.

"I had trained Lee Remick and Angela Lansbury for the show and I didn't want to let them down," he says in William and Jane Stott's *On Broadway.* "I thought the music was grubby and ugly, so I designed an orchestra that was so unusual that it would make the music sound as though there was something really going on. The music was less interesting than it sounded; now it's considered a kind of classic. I read about it years ago; somebody was talking about *Anyone Can Whistle* as being way ahead of its time. And its musical level was such blah, blah, blah, I just howled."

Sniping at the composer wasn't the only problem with *Anyone Can Whistle.* Three songs were cut before rehearsals even began. Another was cut during the Philadelphia run, and one song was written but never used. Everyone sensed something was wrong, but no one could pinpoint it. Everyone started looking for a scapegoat, and it turned out to be Angela.

All of the show's principals already had at least one musical under their belts. Angela's greenhorn status made her an easy target. Charles Adams Baker, her agent at the time, tells it this way:

"They were going to fire Angela in Philadelphia because the whole show didn't work. Very often in the theater, when the show doesn't work, the whipping boy becomes the person who's least experienced. And they said 'Oh, Angela's a movie star; she can't do this.' And she was superb, but they were going to fire her!"

In a brilliant move, Baker contacted another client of his—director/playwright Peter Glenville—who had directed Angela in *Hotel Paradiso.*

"I said 'Somebody has got to pull some weight around here,'"

71

Baker recalls. "We all went and had drinks during the matinee, and Peter, who is terribly authoritative and very Oxonian, told them: 'You have discovered the newest musical comedy queen!' And they said, 'You mean Lee Remick?' 'No,' he said, 'Angela Lansbury.'"

Glenville's persuasion worked. Angela survived the Philadelphia run. Unfortunately, the show did not survive Broadway.

Following all the blood, sweat, and tears, the closing notice after only nine performances was crushing. Angela admits it made her "desperately unhappy for quite a long period of time. We'd poured our hearts and souls into it, and here my forward motion came to a halt."

All was not lost, however. In recognition of just how strong a score Sondheim had written, Columbia Records' president Goddard Lieberson decided to record it, despite the fact that a show usually has to run a minimum number of performances. In recognition of Lieberson's foresight, Stephen Sondheim dedicated the album to him. But imagine the mood of the cast, turning up in the recording studio.

"We did the album on Sunday morning, the day after the Saturday we closed," Angela remembers. "We were all exhausted and depressed."

Still, the show must go on, and once they got into the spirit of the thing, the recording session wasn't so bad. "We were all non-singers," Angela says. "But we had a ball."

She would always remember *Anyone Can Whistle* as a "magnificent failure," but it did some positive things for her in addition to helping her grow as a person and a performer.

"I'd proven myself to producers. I could sing. The show had enhanced my musical talents. I was ready to go to battle again."

Go to battle she would, but not until she'd packed her bags for Hollywood once again, slogged through three more films and even a guest shot on an episode of "The Man From U.N.C.L.E," and outlasted some forty other actresses for the role that was to make her a superstar.

During one of its nine performances, *Anyone Can Whistle* was to count among its audiences a number of Broadway writers and producers. Two of these were Jerome Lawrence and Robert E. Lee, whose hit play *Auntie Mame* was in the process of being turned into a musical by Jerry Herman. Stephen Sondheim's lyrics for "Everybody Says Don't" provide one more bit of prophecy:

> Make just a ripple
> Come on, be brave.
> This time a ripple
> Next time a wave.

Anyone Can Whistle had been the ripple. *Mame* would be the wave.

> *I'm like one of those dandelion seed puffs. I fly around in the air never sure where I'm going to land. You play it by ear, go where the work is and hope some new offer will make you glow a little in anticipation.*

The Amorous Adventures Of Moll Flanders was at least a good time. After months of brooding over the failure of *Whistle,* Angela shook off her depression and went on with her life. This included zipping over to London just before Christmas, 1964 to frolic with an international cast that included Kim Novak, Richard Johnson, old friend George Sanders, Lilli Palmer, Leo McKern, and Vittorio De Sica.

"This movie is not about acting, it's about sex," Angela winked mischievously at one reporter. And she had no objections to, as the critics put it, "going down with the rest of them as a gay milady."

She played Lady Blystone, the daughter of a duke, married to a dissolute and lecherous Vittorio De Sica.

"We're the most exquisitely dressed, destitute, charming wasters of high society," was how she described it. "It's a romp!"

The entire cast's enjoyment of the good dirty fun was apparent in the dailies. Paramount production boss Howard Koch was reportedly so delighted with the rushes he sent cables to London daily, full of praise for cast and crew.

Critics were less enthused. Possibly they were expecting another *Tom Jones,* or at least a film that rang true to the Daniel Defoe novel. Paramount Pictures' version of the tale of a sweet young thing who uses the only talent she has to win over the rich and powerful of eighteenth-century London may have lost something in the transla-

74

tion. Lavish and well-intentioned, it earned this comment from *New York Times* critic Howard Thompson:

"What begins as a briskly bawdy and amusing odyssey of a buffeted, grasping charmer eventually dissolves into pretentious and tedious burlesque."

Thompson did offer some sympathy for what he called a "limber cast." "Professionals like Miss Lansbury, as a twittering peeress . . . have a rough time sledding through to the lighthearted but obvious fade-out."

She was to have an even rougher time sledding through her next movie. Two movies entitled *Harlow* were released in 1965. One was the cheap, technically shoddy Electronovision version, based on Irving Shulman's tattletale bio of the "blond bombshell" of 1930s Hollywood. Starring Carol Lynley, it was surprisingly well-scripted, and actually bore some resemblance to the real story.

Within two months, Paramount Pictures released its own *Harlow*, with Carroll Baker playing the star-crossed starlet. It was an absolute travesty, sanitizing and humanizing all of the demons that drove Jean Harlow to an early grave. In the funeral scene, a character with a remarkable resemblance to Louis B. Mayer remarks, "She didn't die of pneumonia—she died of life." The rest of the dialogue is not much better. One of the demons is Miss Harlow's pushy déclassé mother, played by Angela Lansbury who emerged surprisingly well from the character of Mama Jean. In general the critics acknowledged her struggle with the role and treated her kindly.

Following this episode, Angela managed two significant trips to New York in the spring of 1965. As the rsult of one, she would within the year "dance to a new rhythm, whistle a new song" in a way no one but she would have dreamed possible. As a result of the other, she would wrap up this dreary phase of her movie career with something resembling a warm, sensitive role.

Mister Buddwing was an effort to follow the then-popular trend of amnesia movies, whose entire plot hinged on the central character's accidental loss of memory and his attempts to piece his life back together. Probably the most successful of these was Alfred Hitchcock's *Spellbound*, starring Gregory Peck. *Mister Buddwing* appeared a year later. It was not directed by Hitchcock, and did not star Gregory Peck. Instead it offered movie-goers James Garner as a composer who regains consciousness in Central Park with no idea who he is or how he got there. His only connection to the past is a phone number scribbled on a scrap of paper in his pocket.

Garner is a likeable enough actor, but his style tends to be linear and just this side of "gee whiz." He can hardly be blamed, however, for a meandering script about a syndrome which psychologists claim does not really exist, at least not in the way it is portrayed in movies. In fairness, Garner did the best he could, and so did the rest of the cast.

The phone number in Mr. Buddwing's pocket happens to belong to a middle-aged blonde named Gloria. ". . . a sleepy, somewhat sloppy, but kindhearted blonde dowager who, for no real reason, not only lets him into her apartment but also gives him a handout," as A.H. Weiler described her. The sloppy blonde was none other than Angela. The audience never does find out who Gloria is, or why she helps Buddwing along the way. In general none of the several women in his life are actually identified, and when he is finally reunited with his wife, the audience never sees her.

Dale Wasserman's script from Evan Hunter's novel was a shambles. So was the attempt to shoot it on location in New York. Labor union difficulties added to the general mayhem of shooting in and around New York street crowds, who were not as sophisticated in the presence of movie cameras as they are these days.

Angela gave it her best, though she may have had her mind on other things. Ever since *Anyone Can Whistle* had closed over a year before, she had been in the running for the role that her instincts had always told her was *it*. Hard work and persistence were about to be rewarded for once with a generous dose of luck. And Broadway would never be the same.

> *There were times when I said, "Oh, the hell with them.*
> *I'm not going to worry about that." But I really wanted*
> *it. I couldn't believe that I wasn't going to get it, because it*
> *was so utterly perfect for me. I knew that.*

*I*t should have been obvious. An eccentric, essentially irritating zany like Mame Dennis can only be played successfully by a strong, experienced, versatile character actress, like Angela Lansbury. Only the producers couldn't see it.

Composer/lyricist Jerry Herman's biggest splash had been *Hello, Dolly!* It was the kind of show that was to become his trademark—a one character, one song musical extravaganza. Without a dynamic workhorse of an actress to hold the center together, such a show collapses. Herman and *Hello, Dolly!* had been blessed with Carol Channing. The formula had worked so well she was one of the first to be considered to play Mame.

The Auntie Mame who was to captivate Broadway audiences for 1,508 first-run performances was a far cry from the addle-brained crackpot Patrick Dennis had created in his novel. She was to be far more likeable than the strident Rosalind Russell movie version. This was a plum role, a center stage, in-the-spotlight tour de force that no actress of a certain age could refuse.

And most of them wanted it. Everyone from Lucille Ball to Judy Garland to Elizabeth Taylor employed all of their charm, persuasion, and considerable influence on producers Fryer, Carr, and Harris, and composer Herman. Rosalind Russell and Mary Martin, by contrast, turned it down. Ethel Merman, to whom it was offered on a platter, was too exhausted after the run of *Gypsy* and reluctantly said no.

All of them had more box office clout than Angela, who was known as a second-luminary movie star. Through the auspices of old friend Jerome Lawrence, one of the show's cowriters who had seen what she could do in *Anyone Can Whistle*, Angela begged Jerry Herman for an audition. She flew to New York and got the audition, but nothing else. Jerry Herman remembers it this way.

"I suggested to Jerome Lawrence and Bob Lee that we get this lady, who was an actress who could sing. I got together with this lady and taught her one song, 'It's Today,' and she got the part."

Mr. Herman's hindsight is commendable, but the facts stack up somewhat differently. Despite his and Jerome Lawrence's convictions that this was the actress they wanted, the producers resisted. They weren't indifferent enough to turn Angela down completely, but they did keep her waiting for nearly a year while they auditioned some forty other actresses. In that amount of time Angela's emotional investment in *Mame* went from mild interest to major obsession.

"If I couldn't work, I spent my time doing other things that pleased me just as well," she remembers. "Things with my children, gardening, ordinary hand things."

She credits Peter with getting her "off her behind" and forcing her to strive for this role against all odds.

"I was a wife and a mother, and I was completely fulfilled. But my husband recognized the signals in me which said 'I've been doing enough gardening, I've cooked enough good dinners, I've sat around the house and mooned about what more interior decoration I can get my fingers into.' It's a curious thing with actors and actresses, but suddenly the alarm goes off. My husband is a very sensitive person to my moods and he recognized the fact that I had to get on with something. *Mame* came along out of the blue just at this time. Now isn't that a miracle?"

Every time she read the script in that year of waiting, her interest grew. "I knew this would be a success the minute I heard the title," she confesses. "*Mame* had the material to take off like a bird."

The story goes that it was director Gene Saks (*Enter Laughing* and *Nobody Loves An Albatross*) who held out against Angela. Finally she decided she wasn't going to wait any longer. Without naming names, she can talk about her anger and how she finally told them to put up or shut up.

"I was exasperated and hurt—by that time I was absolutely hurt—because I felt I had extended myself, that I'd done my bit, and they couldn't have the decency to make up their minds. So I said, 'Either tell me now, or I'm going to go home, and I'll forget about it. But don't keep me hanging around any longer. It's not fair.'"

At last they caved in. Angela went on a crash diet, shed twelve pounds and came out high-kicking. *Mame* was hers and she was Mame. The role would be linked with her from then on, no matter who else played it. Her time had come.

A blur of rehearsals and fittings for the twenty-four costume changes quickly followed. From a homebound "cabbage" who cooked and sewed and gardened and took her kids backpacking in the High Sierras, she was being transformed into a superstar.

Ever practical, the first thing she did once she was comfortably ensconced in New York was unpack her favorite teapot and prescribe her own "high energy" diet. Steak, asparagus tips and unflavored gelatin became her staples. Dessert was rhubarb and vanilla ice cream, with a glass of burgundy "for the blood." She also seriously tried to quit smoking for the first time in her life. She was going to need all the wind she could muster to belt through her nine musical numbers (out of thirteen) in the show. In addition she had to dance her way through a tango, a cakewalk and a Charleston without missing a beat.

"I survived the London blitz," she told *Daily News* columnist Robert Wahls breathlessly. "Quite possibly I can survive all this."

Opening night loomed less than three weeks away. Angela would not only have to survive it, she would have to stretch, reach inside herself, and find an energy level she had never used before. She was giving life to a brand new character on a grand scale, but she didn't let it throw her. The story of the Manhattan socialite who adopts her orphaned nephew and gives him a most unorthodox education was something Angela could easily identify with.

"Mame is for me," she said emphatically. "She's a wise woman, a teacher. She always has a new horizon. She wants to get her orphaned nephew out of the rut most people live in. And she wants to give the greatest gift, love of life and living. Yes, she's capricious, but honest. She's a realist."

"I'm called Mame as often as Angela," she would tell one columnist near the end of the two-year run. "People expect me to be Mame Dennis. In their minds I am, and they don't, as often as not, separate the star from the role."

If the transition appeared effortless, it was only because Angela is such a pro. In actuality, as anyone who has ever done eight shows a week can verify, it was grueling, back-breaking work.

"The one thing God gave me is energy," Angela declared. "Playing Mame is like being a track star. People out front have no idea of the endurance you need."

Angela endured. Her opening number was "It's Today." And on May 24, 1966, it *was*.

"When the people got tired of whistling and clapping like thunder, they stood up in the newly refurbished Winter Garden and screamed," Rex Reed reported in the *New York Times*. "As Mame, Angela Lansbury is a happy caterpillar, turning—after years of being nose-thumbed in Hollywood in endless roles as baggy-faced frumps—into a gilt-edged butterfly."

Opening night was pandemonium of the best kind—the chaos of success. One could feel it in the air, like static electricity. *Mame* was a hit, and so was Angela.

"*Mame* is replete with lively song and dance, an exceptionally able cast, and a splendidly splashy production. Even the scenery was entertaining," *Times* drama critic Stanley Kaufmann wrote. "This star vehicle deserves its star, and vice is very much versa. No one can be surprised to learn that Angela Lansbury is an accomplished actress, but not all of us may know that she has an adequate singing voice, can dance trimly, and can combine all these matters into musical performance."

Richard Watts of the *New York Post* was somewhat less enthusiastic, but equally willing to give credit where it was due. "My own rapture was plainly far more modified than that of the ecstatic audience," he wrote, "though the entire enterprise is deserving of the approval it is sure to receive. Angela Lansbury, in a role that keeps her constantly active, plays with humor and charm and sings excellently."

Box office figures supported everyone's prognosis. In a time when a Broadway ticket could be had for one-fifth of its present cost, *Mame* did $22,000 in ticket sales on opening night. "Angela Lansbury and *Mame* have settled into a big smash," the *New York Post* reported happily.

Backstage the pandemonium was complete. In a tiny white dressing room with dark blue carpet two flights above the stage, a barefoot, exuberant Angela welcomed all comers. Her husband Peter, whom Rex Reed described as looking like "a Mississippi riverboat gambler in an old Tyrone Power movie," offered Scotch in paper cups to all and sundry from a refrigerator stocked with seltzer, frozen orange juice and a bouquet of gardenias from an admirer. There was no furniture except for the dressing table; people milled around— hugging, kissing, sharing the moment. A Hirschfeld cartoon showing Mame sitting on the moon, celebrating the "Man in the Moon" number from the show, shared the walls with other theater caricatures. Well-wishers from Bea Arthur and director Gene Saks to agents and critics and her old director from *Dorian Gray*, Albert Lewin, stopped by to congratulate Angela. Lewin sat holding her hands and reminiscing about her singing "Little Yellow Bird" in *Dorian Gray*, and how far she had come since.

Then it was off to Sardi's in an air conditioned limousine, wending her way through a crowd of fans packing the sidewalk outside the Winter Garden chanting "Angela! Angela!" in the warm spring Broadway night.

There was another crowd waiting to cheer her outside Sardi's, and the "in" crowd waiting inside to greet her sweeping entrance with warm applause. Angela stopped to chat with the headwaiter, who had promised to pray to St. Jude for *Mame*'s success. Angela thanked him for his prayers; if she knew St. Jude was the patron saint of hopeless causes, she was too gracious to mention it. Feasting on strawberries and cream, she signed endless autographs, and welcomed the comments of gushing fans and drunken mashers alike.

"She's all heart," Peter Shaw sighed, always trying to look out for the lady he loved. "She'll let the biggest bores in the world bend her ear all night and feel so sorry for them she'll invite them for breakfast the next morning."

"How can I tell you what a staggering victory *Mame* is for me?" Angela bubbled. "I always suspected I could reach everybody, but I never did until now. I've finally found a role that is the sum total of everything I know and everybody's digging me for the first time."

The icing on the cake was when the management at Sardi's had her old Hirschfeld caricature from *A Taste Of Honey* moved into the restaurant's front room. Before it had languished in oblivion in the back room near the kitchen. Now it and Angela were back in the spotlight.

But even the giddiness of opening night was overshadowed by an incident that seemed minor at the time. The kids had flown to New York with Peter to share their mother's big night. At three o'clock in the morning, after the party at Sardi's, fourteen-year-old Anthony had to be rushed to a hospital emergency room. The official story was that he had an infected finger which became so badly swollen he had to have a ring removed, but this may have been only partly true.

The truth about their children's involvement in the drug scene and the horrors Angela and Peter lived through in the late sixties were not made public until years later. But by the time *Mame* gave his mother her moment of hard-won glory, Anthony was already on his way to serious trouble. As an adult, he talks about it with quiet detachment.

"I started when I was twelve. I smoked grass and sniffed a lot of strange glues at first, but then I graduated to pills, both uppers and downers. By the time I was fifteen I was on both cocaine and heroin. I thought it was glamorous."

"Malibu was a hotbed of youthful drug abuse," Angela can say now, looking back on those painful years. "To those kids it was as common as bubblegum. Both my children, but particularly my son, became involved."

Angela was not the kind of mother to stand idly by and wring her hands. Her own too-brief childhood had taught her to be tough.

83

When it was obvious that *Mame* would run for a good long time, she pulled the kids out of the dangerous west coast environment, enrolling them in a private school in Manhattan and insisting they stay with her. Meanwhile, she guarded her family's privacy like a tigress.

"It's a bit of a wrench for them to leave California and their friends and school and the activities they love," was all she would tell reporters about why she wanted Anthony and Deirdre with her. "But they're going to have to face it. I regret uprooting the children, but that's the sort of thing everyone must learn to accept about life. They're a little upset, but very gutsy," she added, defending her kids' individuality as she had all their lives.

A nightmare of psychiatrists and private drug treatment centers, of partial successes and heartbreaking setbacks, was already beginning. Meanwhile, Angela had to go on with the rest of her life.

No one who hasn't survived a similar experience can imagine how painful it must have been for her. Here she was, night after night, playing a kind of super-parent to her young stage nephew Patrick, while battling doubts about her success as a mother to her real children. When drama critic Stanley Kaufmann said of Mame, "The visceral test, I suppose, is whether one is jealous of little Patrick growing up with an aunt like that. I was green," the irony must have been particularly painful.

She had been born to act; it was in her blood. Should she have given up her career when the children were born? Or, like too many Hollywood mothers of her generation, should she have shunted them off to the care of strangers and ignored them? She had tried to give herself to her children *and* her career. Had she somehow done it wrong?

There had been some chaos when the children were small and she'd had to juggle her career around them. But she'd always turned down work that would take her out of Hollywood and away from them for too long. But there'd been the times she'd had to fly to New York for a day or two of quick television work to fill in when there was nothing else available. Had her erratic schedule planted the seeds of an insecurity that would later drive her children to drugs? She had always tried to let her children be themselves. In doing so, had she given them too much freedom at too early an age?

On the other hand, had it been a mistake to bring the children to New York during her two previous Broadway runs, a mistake to separate them from their friends, substitute private tutors for school, "grown-up" parties and restaurant dinners for outings with their peers and at-home family holidays?

Over the next several years she would have to come to terms with her doubts and realize that she had done the best she could. And in the final analysis, all the psychiatrists and treatment centers couldn't accomplish what one determined mother would.

> *With each audience I feel I am communicating, telling them something I want them to know.* Mame *does people so much good.*
>
> *I had no idea of what happens to the star of a smash Broadway musical. No one could have told me. I haven't the push that drives actresses to the front. I don't know how successful I am; it worries me a little.*

The raves continued throughout the run of *Mame*. No one had seen anything quite like Angela.

"Miss Lansbury is a singing-dancing actress, not a singer or dancer who also acts," was how Stanley Kaufmann defined the talent and training that made her special. "There is even more character color in her singing than in her spoken dialogue. In this marathon role she has wit, poise, warmth, and a very taking coolth."

When *Mame* had been running for almost two years, Robert Wahls of the New York *Daily News* quipped, tongue-in-cheek, "What was this fortyish blond up to coming on as a Broadway musical comedy star, a species rare as the whooping crane? Could she even sell tickets?"

In June of 1966, Angela's rarity was rewarded with the first of her four Tony Awards.

There are three audiences whose approval any Broadway actor craves. First of course is the ticket-buying audience; their collective love thundering across the lights every night is like nothing else on this earth. The second audience is the critics; without their support no show can survive. And third, but not least, is the approval of one's fellow actors; the Antoinette Perry Award is concrete proof of that approval.

Stumbling up to accept her award, Angela found her eyes filled with tears. She could barely speak. She stuttered out her breathless thanks, and in a trembling voice managed to say, "You are looking at an actress who, until now, has always been a successful nominee."

This simple speech won her that night's audience, too.

Mame also received two other Tonys that year. Bea Arthur won Best Supporting Actress as the raucous, boozy Vera Charles, and Best Supporting Actor went to little Frankie Michaels as Mame's nephew Patrick.

Mame brought it all together for Angela. Her faith in herself and in her destiny had finally been fulfilled. Her natural serenity, her ability to wait, had paid off.

"I'm a true Libran," is how she puts it. "I wait, I weigh, I see both points of view. I'm thankful that while I waited for a part like Mame I kept my hand in as an actress without settling for doing substandard material anywhere along the line. Whether I did or did not make it in the big way that I have certainly does not alter the fact that I have had a very rich, full life, and a very happy one in almost every area except complete stardom."

Having achieved that stardom with *Mame,* she realized that for once she had some real control over her future. At an age when most actresses can only look back on their best years, she had it all ahead of her.

"Women of my age are coming into their own," she told May Okon of the *Daily News.* "We are no longer the older generation to our youngsters. I hope that because of *Mame* I will be able to go back to movies and possibly move into a new era of roles for a woman of my age, roles of a leading nature in which I can portray exciting and attractive mature women, and start a whole new trend."

The prophecy of that last sentence would not be fulfilled until eighteen years later—not in movies but in, of all things, a prime time television series. "Murder, She Wrote" would offer her precisely the kind of "exciting and attractive mature woman" she wanted to play. In the most youth-obsessed medium, an attractive, mature Jessica Fletcher would consistently capture third place in the Neilsen ratings. And an attractive, mature Angela Lansbury would become the most recognized female face on television.

But the strong sense of self that would carry her through the intervening years was already hers during *Mame.* After nearly eight hundred performances, she relinquished the role to Janis Paige. Several big name stars were anxious to take over the run, but Angela recommended Janis, and by now she had enough clout to have her recommendation taken seriously.

She took only one vacation from *Mame.* Turning the role over to Celeste Holm in August, 1967, she flew to Reno to meet Peter and the children. They drove to Lake Tahoe for a glorious two weeks of hiking and camping on Emerald Bay. It was a necessary escape from the rigors of Broadway, and a way to keep in touch with her children's needs.

Deirdre and Anthony had stayed in New York with her for nearly a year, but their sense of disorientation, of not belonging, was so strong that Angela had reluctantly sent them back to Malibu, trusting Peter to "hold the fort" in her prolonged absence. It was an uneasy compromise, an effort to solve what she calls "the unhappiness."

"Being the star of *Mame* was a joy, but behind the facade I'd find Anthony in my dressing room, tormented, asking for an advance on his allowance. We both knew what it was for."

As if to take her mind off her personal heartaches, Angela plunged into a number of public appearances and charitable endeavors. Thanksgiving, 1966 found her as a guest star on a Perry Como television special. In May of 1967 she was crowned Queen of the Peacock Ball at a benefit for the Lila Motley Cancer Foundation of NYU Medical Center held at the Plaza Hotel. The following month she attended the March of Dimes Annual Benefit Luncheon as its guest of honor.

There were purely social events too. Angela became an almost frenetic party-goer. At a party given by Ruth Ford and Rex Reed for musician Bobby Short at The Living Room, columnist Earl Wilson remarked that she was wearing "the shortest micro-skirt in the place." Avoiding personal questions, Angela talked about her recent decision to turn down the title role in the controversial *Killing Of Sister George,* a role she felt would not enhance her public image. "It was not an easy decision to make," she assured Wilson.

She went on to chat about the national tour of *Mame,* scheduled for mid-1968, and steered the conversation toward that evening's performance.

"The King of Nepal and a party of twenty-five are coming in tonight," she said, as if she couldn't quite believe it herself. "I hope the king leaves a nice little ruby behind for everybody."

On March 29, 1968, the cast of *Mame* threw a party at the Ground Floor restaurant following Angela's last performance. Within a month she would take most of them with her on a limited tour, starting with a tryout in Philadelphia, followed by seven weeks each in San Francisco and Los Angeles.

The Los Angeles run was particularly important to her. She had relinquished a longer Broadway run and a London tour in order to "show them" in L.A. This was the town she had called home since she was seventeen years old. She had left Hollywood an also-ran and was coming back a star. How would audiences react to her?

New York Times L.A. correspondent Robert Windeler said it all in a column headlined: "ANGELA LANSBURY A HIT IN COAST MAME."

"It isn't often that a movie actress goes to Broadway to become a big star; it's even rarer when she has a chance to come back to Hollywood and show the skeptics in her home town how and why she did it."

On opening night at the Pavilion of the Los Angeles Music Center, a 3,243-member capacity audience showed Angela exactly how they felt. They stood as a body and gave her a twenty-minute ovation. Broadway's very own Dolly, Carol Channing, was in the audience that night. She called the performance "an unforgettable triumph for Angie in every way."

Meanwhile, Warner Bros.-Seven Arts had acquired the film rights to *Mame* for three and one-half million dollars. While Angela may have seemed the obvious choice to repeat her portrayal on film, spokesmen for Warner's would only give her a fifty-fifty chance. Too many others, many of them the same actresses who had jostled for the role on Broadway, were too interested in it for Warner to tip its hand. Angela remained very cool about it.

"I could get my fix on doing the movie, wangle my way into it somehow and then have it turn out to be all wrong." She was going to let come what may. Ultimately, of course, it was Lucille Ball who wangled her way into the movie. Considering the outcome, Angela was better off out of it.

But basking in the L.A. audiences' nightly ovations, she didn't have time to worry. Something else was already in the works. After a three-week vacation, she committed to another Jerry Herman project. The man who may or may not have "discovered" her for Mame had gathered together many of the principals from that show for his newest musical, *Dear World*.

Dear World was a perfect example of the fact that there is no magic formula to guarantee the success of a Broadway musical. In an attempt to capitalize on the success of *Mame*, Jerry Herman, Jerome Lawrence and Robert E. Lee took Maurice Vallency's adaptation of Jean Girardoux's novel *The Madwoman of Chaillot* and tried to turn it into a musical. Their problems were manifold right from the start.

The story line might have worked. The success of both the novel and the straight play suggested that there was some appeal left in this fairy tale of a crackpot old lady living in the Paris sewers and championing the poor and the downtrodden by fancifully murdering financiers and wealthy speculators. To stretch a point, Countess Aurelia wasn't all that different from Mame in her sense of injustice, her choice of oddball friends, and her idea of a good time. But where Mame was an eccentric, Countess Aurelia was an outright loony, and Angela played her that way. It didn't help that she and the rest of the cast were left stranded with a tired book and monotonous lyrics.

Jerry Herman's obsession with title songs had begun with *Hello,*

Dolly! and was to evolve through *Mame* and *Dear World* to *Mack and Mabel.* But one song does not an entire musical make, even when the audience leaves the theater humming it. Audiences hummed "Hello, Dolly!" and "Mame." They didn't bother with "Dear World."

As for the script, Clive Barnes said, "The Lawrence and Lee book has a well-worn air to it, as if it had been rewritten more times than Soviet history and probably cannot quite believe that it is still there. The dialogue exerts a plodding price for its few moments of grace."

Troubles under the heading of "artistic differences" dogged the show from its Boston tryout through the New York opening. First-time director Lucia Victor was let go and much of her groundwork restaged by veteran Peter Glenville. According to Jerry Herman, "I, Miss Lansbury, Mr. Lee, and Mr. Lawrence differed with Miss Victor over interpretation."

Angela was not available for comment then, but she was sufficiently vocal after the endless changes between Boston and New York resulted in an almost unrecognizable show.

"Problems started very early in the game," she remembers. "*Dear World* was written as a small, intimate musical, and I promise you that the show we opened with in Boston had far more quality in the first five minutes than we ever achieved with all the changes."

Nevertheless, Boston audiences had been surprisingly lukewarm. Angela, always the practical one, tended to think she was the wrench in the works.

"We tried to please the audience who expected me to come out and do high kicks. They didn't want to see me playing a seventy-five-year-old lady with lots of makeup. It was one of the most difficult times I've had in the theater. I was appalled and very shocked at the audience's reaction in Boston, and it was only because I was doing it. I really do believe that I was a deterrent to the success of the show simply because of the audience's prior conception of me. If it had been anybody else, it would have made it."

Critics were far kinder to her than she was to herself. Most of them found her the show's one saving grace. Richard Watts, Jr., under the headline "Trapped in the Paris Sewers," wrote in the *New*

York Post, "So much hard work and so many weeks of industrious previews have gone into the making of *Dear World,* but despite a picturesque performance by Angela Lansbury, the result is disappointingly mediocre. The mad countess is so buried in grotesque makeup that there is little of the handsome Miss Lansbury left, but her skill and vitality are still there, and she is the evening's major blessing."

In the *Times,* Clive Barnes was even crueller toward *Dear World,* kinder to Angela. "For the most part [*Dear World*] stubbornly refuses to get off the ground, except when it is delicately flounced airborne by a delicate kick from the adorable Miss Lansbury, who not only can make magic out of nothing but has to. But for one minor miracle I suspect that *Dear World* would never have seen the gloom of day. The minor miracle is Miss Lansbury and whether or not the musical itself is worth seeing—for it is extraordinarily tenuous—no connoisseur of musical comedy can afford to miss Miss Lansbury's performance. It is lovely."

The situation backstage also earned mixed reviews. Less than two weeks into the New York run, some of it hit the press.

"Backstage at the Mark Hellinger, unhappiness reigns," the *New York Post* reported, pleased at having some "dirt" to report on a star whose career had been notoriously free of scandal. "Angela Lansbury, who got some nice reviews for her role, wants out. And the rest of the cast is feuding with Angela. They claim she behaved like a virago, insisting on multiple changes in the play out of town. Angela, on her part, insists that the musical, which was faring badly with audiences in Boston, needed them."

On the surface, this might seem credible. It wouldn't be the first time the star of a show in trouble tried to bail out from a simple sense of self-preservation. But Angela is not a quitter, not someone to pull superstar tantrums. Having been through so much in her own career, she would not jeopardize others' by trying to pull out of a show that so many people were depending on. And she continued to maintain that the Boston show was better than the New York one; it was not she who made the changes.

The *Post* story needs to be taken with a grain of salt and with an understanding of what else was going on in Angela's life at the time. Anthony's drug problem was growing increasingly worse. His parents had despaired of helping him themselves, and had had him committed to a private treatment center in Los Angeles. Every time he was given a few days' leave he would seek out his connections and go back on drugs. He was doing heroin and cocaine and occasionally LSD. There didn't seem to be anything his parents could do whether they were with him or, as Angela was, stranded on the opposite coast in a show everybody seemed to hate.

Situations like this make any artist question the value of what she is trying to do with her life. Is it any wonder that Angela, caught in trivial differences of opinion in her onstage life, helpless to control the important things in her offstage life, might have been snappish with cast and crew?

Finally it got down to money. Producer Alexander Cohen was quoted as saying he would not close the show unless box office receipts went below $51,000 a week. The Mark Hellinger had a potential to gross $104,000 per week and, according to *Variety*, actually did $74,000 the first week. So, with the house less than three-quarters full, the show went on. And it won Angela her second Tony.

"I just prefer what turns out to be good entertainment, you know," Angela told a reporter following the awards ceremony, trying to put a brave face on it. "I am always delighted when I get lost in a show, when I forget I am in a theater. That seldom happens."

Small wonder, considering what was going on at home. Still, Angela wasn't about to air her sorrows in public. Deflecting any personal questions, she went on to explain her philosophy of theater.

"Our minds need to be romanced, our ears need to be lulled, otherwise why are we there?"

And some of the old spunk was still there.

"Somebody asked me about the Living Theater," she commented drily on the "let-it-all-hang-out" school of acting that was popular in the late sixties. "Well, it makes no sense to me at all. It sounds like a sort of therapy. But don't lump it in with our theater, you know."

94

Dear World ran for 132 performances and then faded quietly into oblivion. It was, as Gerald Bordman characterized it in *American Musical Theater,* an "interesting failure."

Afterward Angela felt that she might have done enough theater for the present. It was time to try the movies again. She had been offered a project that seemed to have everything she needed—a glamorous leading role in which she could prove that life didn't have to end at forty, a European location, and Hal Prince, a most unusual theater director making his movie dircctorial debut.

And most important, it would give her a chance to pull her kids out of the drug haven of Malibu and keep them with her on location in a small Bavarian village throughout the summer. She hoped in this way to break the grip of the illness that now possessed them both.

The film was to go through innumerable title changes. Considering what she hoped that summer would provide for her and her children, Angela would certainly have seen the final release title as a good omen. That title was *Something For Everyone.*

> *The thirties were a bit rough. The forties are marvelous—I really enjoy them tremendously. I felt much older when I was thirty-six—I worried more about being thirty-six—than I did when I was forty. Men are very interested in you when you are forty—more so than when you are thirty-six.*

While she was talking about her personal life, Angela might have been summing up the plot of *Something For Everyone* with that quote. The premise of a fading countess who has lost her fortune, lives in a cottage on the grounds of her decaying castle, and is seduced by a former servant may have seemed a bit lush, but it had excellent credentials.

Based on a novel by Harry Kressing, the film was first called *The Dreamers*. During the course of shooting it was to undergo several reincarnations, first as *The Rook*, then as *Today The Castle* and finally *Something For Everyone*. Each title says something about the film, but the number of changes suggests an ambivalence in the production.

The ambivalence was obvious to the critics. Vincent Canby called the film "a comic parable about the rise of 'that dreadful little house-painter' . . . cast in the form of a contemporary fairy tale." And there was something unreal about the mysterious stranger, played by Michael York, who deftly seduces first the son and then the mother in this decadent aristocratic family.

Possibly the locale bred a kind of unreality. The film was shot on location at Hohenschwangen, Fussen, Bavaria, a quaint little toy town three thousand feet up in the Bavarian Alps, just downwind from Neuschwanstein Castle. In the nineteenth century, Neuschwanstein Castle was the home of a prince known as Mad Ludwig, who was seized by the citizenry and drowned for running the entire province into bankruptcy.

With this sort of lunacy in the air, *Something For Everyone* may have tried to be an art film, but the end result was only partially successful. Maybe Harold Prince's background got in the way. The director of such Broadway hits as *Baker Street, Cabaret, Zorba,* and the later *Company* may have tried to apply his hit-making theatrical technique to film. It didn't work. Vincent Canby summed it up this way:

"I kept expecting *Something For Everyone* to break into cynical song. It is made tolerable, much like some big, bad Broadway musical, by a kind of surface chic, by mechanical dexterity, and by occasional funny lines."

Some of the funnier of those lines fell to Angela. As the Countess Herthe von Ornstein, refusing to accept the fact of her family's poverty, she is wont to say, "Rats and house squirrels adapt. Eagles in cages don't adapt—they sit on their perches and glare."

But real people in real life don't often say things like that. And there is much in the larger-than-life premise of *Something For Everyone* that reads like a Broadway musical. A former servant manipulates an entire family—by arranging marriages and murders—in order to restore the family fortune, in the hope that he will get a large chunk of that fortune. This plot is reminiscent of *Sweeney Todd* in its implausibility. It might work if set to music and accompanied by lavish production numbers. Presented straight on a movie screen, it becomes, finally, what Vincent Canby called "summer camp."

The *Times* critic was not above taking Angela to task, either. Harking back to her musical comedy career, he remarks, "Miss Lansbury, instead of reading her lines, is inclined to belt them."

But there is affection in his criticism when he questions her decision to play this "kind of Bette Davis version" of a German countess. "Because I still remember with joy the plump, sad little barmaid of *The Picture of Dorian Gray,* I'm probably the only man in New York who hasn't been transported by Miss Lansbury's later metamorphosis as the queen of Broadway shows apotheosizing the eccentric, middle-aged female that she now brings to the screen."

Neglecting to consider the history of under-appreciation that brought Angela to this point in her career, Canby nevertheless acknowledged her ability to pull off a character in the midst of this sordid little story, which was released in Europe under the title *Black Flowers For The Bride*.

Angela had chosen to do *Something For Everyone* for motives not entirely related to the script, mostly the joy of having her family with her. Peter was able to free up his schedule at William Morris for the summer. His son David, Angela's stepson, now twenty-five, had just returned from service with the Army in Vietnam. The peace and quiet of the little Alpine village was especially necessary for him. A troubled Anthony, age seventeen, and Deirdre, sixteen, had a chance to escape the pressure cooker of Hollywood. Angela must have known bringing them to Europe was only a holding action, but she lived in hope.

There was something in it for her, too. Despite her statements about how much fun it was to be forty, some little nagging doubt about her age and her chances for the future must have crept in. Maybe *Mame* had been it—her one big splash, never to be repeated. *Something For Everyone* gave her a chance to dress up again, to play act, to, as she told columnist Earl Wilson, "climb out of my knitting bag and get into a bikini again."

Her reasons for *Something For Everyone* were many. It is hard to say *what* her reasons were for doing *Bedknobs and Broomsticks*.

Certain roles haunt actors. James O'Neill, classical actor and father of playwright Eugene O'Neill, played the Count of Monte Cristo for more than twenty-five years. Bela Lugosi had himself buried in his Dracula costume, so completely had the role taken him over. Christopher Plummer, international Shakespearean actor with over thirty Broadway credits alone, is known to Middle America only as the singing Baron von Trapp from *The Sound of Music*. And Leonard Nimoy may never entirely put aside his Spock ears.

Miss Eglantine Price almost had the same effect on Angela. Up until her success in "Murder, She Wrote," millions who had never been to Broadway and never heard of *Mame* remembered her only as the wide-eyed apprentice witch in *Bedknobs and Broomsticks*.

Maybe it was just because no one can refuse a Disney film. Maybe it was the sense of roots offered by the setting in pre-World War II England. Maybe it was the escape offered by a lighthearted family film, a chance to sing and mug and steal scenes from the animators. Maybe it was a refuge from the impossibility of the situation at home. Whatever the reasons, Angela found herself in old-age makeup again, trying her hand at magic.

Bedknobs and Broomsticks was strictly Mary Poppins country revisited, with an older surrogate mother figure in the person of Miss Price, a rural English spinster learning witchcraft through a correspondence course. She has just mastered the art of making her bed fly and is about to graduate to broomsticks when World War II and the London blitz visit her with three evacuee children.

With the aid of the inimitable Disney animators, Miss Price and her charges ride their broomstick to London, to the magical mystical island of Namboombu in search of further magic, and to a soccer game complete with a talking tiger in the grandstand. Five musical numbers by the songwriting Sherman brothers, and a plan to use magic to send guns and planes to fight wars by themselves without soldiers, made this film a romp.

But critics questioned whether the plot might be over the heads of the children the film was aimed at.

"*Bedknobs And Broomsticks* is a tricky, cheerful, aggressively friendly Walt Disney fantasy for children who still find enchantment in pop-up books," Vincent Canby wrote. "I suspect the movie will be something of a long, uninterrupted sit for the very children for whom it's intended, and an even longer one for those parents and guardians who will probably accompany them."

He did praise the special effects though, particularly "an underwater ballet in which Miss Lansbury and [David] Tomlinson dance in slow-motion surrounded by cartoon fish."

Frances Herridge of the *New York Post* said, "[*Bedknobs*] has a great deal going for it, mainly the no-nonsense tone of Angela Lansbury at the most magical nonsense conceivable."

Of Angela's performance, Canby observed, "Miss Lansbury can't help projecting a certain healthy sensuality, even in the most proper Disney circumstances."

Clearly she was no prim and proper Mary Poppins. She did, however, always ride her broom sidesaddle. "Technically," according to her witchcraft manual, "A witch is always a lady."

The broomstick ride over, Angela came back to reality. Before the year was out, that reality was to include Anthony's near-death from an overdose, and the devastating Malibu fire. Angela's world was falling apart.

Peter and I were the typical Eisenhower-years couple during the fifties. But the 1960s were shattering to us as a family. It really shocked me because I didn't think it could happen to my own.

Watching a son being taken away by ambulance in a coma from a heroin overdose would destroy most mothers. Angela survived it because she had to. But even today, with her children long cured and leading meaningful adult lives, she can scarcely bring herself to talk about it. The scars remain.

"The year 1970 was a bad one for us, struggling to help Anthony rid himself of that terrible dependence," she will say, her voice none too steady, those huge blue eyes edged with tears. "I don't think I quite faced it at the time. I postponed it. You have to get through the day, which you fill up dealing with mechanics, new shoes, something to wear besides what's on your back.

"The sadness!" she says, echoing the cry of any parent who has lived through the experience. "If you dwell on it, you wouldn't stop crying for a week. It's still lurking there."

There was anger as well as sadness. Anger at herself for not understanding how she had failed, anger at her son for causing her and Peter so much pain.

"There was a temptation to say to Tony, 'How can you kick your father and me in the face after all the patience and understanding we have given you?' I had to realize he was not doing it to get at me. During the lucid periods he always talked about recovery."

Anthony's hospitalization brought the crisis to a head. Angela and Peter had to face the fact that despite years of psychiatric treatment their son had almost died. Strung out on heroin and cocaine, the tall, handsome eighteen-year-old had wasted away to a skeletal one hundred and twenty pounds. And Deirdre, while not as dramatically in crisis, was also hurting. Bright, beautiful, musically gifted, she was nonetheless fast following her brother down the road to destruction.

Angela fought back like a tigress. That characteristic Lansbury fearlessness threw aside the fancy shrinks and sought a better solution. She would not work again, she would not rest again, until she found somewhere her children could be free.

As it happened, fate handed her a solution, in the form of a disaster.

The brushfires that swept through Malibu and much of southern Los Angeles in the fall of 1970 are legend even today. The firestorm devastated thousands of acres of forest and private land, indiscriminately razing movie-star mansions and smaller homes alike. The Shaws' "Japanese house" was among the casualties.

"We lost the entire contents of the house when it burned," Angela recalls, "including all my letters, diaries and photos and memorabilia from every film I made."

But even with the fire raging out of control all around her, she didn't panic. Typically Angela, she took a practical approach to the crisis.

"I put two metal file cabinets in the Japanese pond, thinking a fire wouldn't travel across water, stupid me. Everything went— passports, the children's birth certificates, everything."

Months and even years of red tape would have to be gone through before important documents could be duplicated.

"But people were very kind," Angela notes. "They even had copies made of all the awards I've won."

Nevertheless, the fire was an omen. That phase of her family's life was over. It was time to move on, to begin again.

"Everything was telling me to take my family and get away, so I did."

Within a week she and Peter had purchased an old parsonage in county Cork, Ireland.

"It was one of the happiest decisions of my life. It was one of the last places on earth that was fairly drug free. It was also a spiritual home for me."

The spiritual home was necessary for the whole family, but most especially for Angela. She had felt like a gypsy ever since she'd left England during the blitz. No matter how long she'd stayed in New York, it had never felt like home. And while she'd tried to put down roots in Malibu, it was now associated with so many bad memories that it was best left behind.

"California holds only unpleasant memories," Angela said at the time. "Once we kicked the sand out of our shoes, we lost all nostalgia for the place. I wanted to see the bogs and hills again, and after the fire wiped us out I wanted to start life over again in an uncluttered way and live a simple life." She described the Irish homestead not as an escape but as "a strategic retreat."

In the middle of twenty rolling, fallow acres on the Bride River in rural county Cork, the Shaws' retreat was an 1820s ivy-covered Georgian-style farmhouse with stone staircases and a big country kitchen. Angela, who has always believed the kitchen to be the heart of any home, set to work creating a dream home.

"We tore up the entire cellar and put in a dream kitchen. Everybody in the family cooks. It's nest-building time in a way."

The nest-building included cleaning out and refurbishing the stone fireplaces in every room and designing a stereo system where music could be piped through the entire house using the natural acoustics of the two-story stone staircase. Angela, the passionate gardener, planted three dozen rosebushes and started a vegetable and berry garden. Her first season's yield included lettuce, spinach, asparagus, strawberries, and over forty pounds of raspberries.

Most importantly, the family was together. In 1972 Peter retired from the William Morris Agency to become Angela's full time manager. Deirdre, with a new lease on life, began to study painting. Anthony was given a choice: stay behind in California and watch his life go down the drain, or come to Ireland and stay clean.

In short, Angela discovered Tough Love long before anyone else invented it. She set her son to hard manual labor, renovating the house and building fieldstone walls with his bare hands. If the fresh air and backbreaking work couldn't exorcise her son's demons, nothing could. Following her own philosophy, she also romanced his mind.

"Mum was wonderful," Anthony remembers. "She drove me all over Ireland, pointing out the sights, and she bought me boxes of books to keep my mind occupied. I went through hell during the withdrawal period. I took up hard labor, getting my weight up again from a hundred and twenty pounds to a hundred and eighty."

Angela didn't realize it at first, but her special brand of therapy was working on *her* as well. The temptation to stay where she was, amid the lilacs and the three-hundred-year-old elm trees, to putter around in the garden in baggy sweaters, to drink tea, and to make her own strawberry jam for the rest of her life was almost overpowering. The soul-soothing sound of the River Bride meandering gently out back, the sight of the cows coming up from the glen every evening, the bells around their necks ringing in the still air, the leisurely walks through the rolling countryside to watch the steeplechase horses and the newborn lambs on the neighboring farms offered more peace and tranquility than anyone could ask for. The two Tonys on the mantle in the parlor may have reminded her of old glories, but for the moment she didn't miss them. Her trips to New York these days were solely for the purpose of buying essentials like doorknobs and waxed paper. Angela was in danger of becoming a cabbage again. But for the moment, she was a happy cabbage.

As if the fire and the children's drug problems weren't enough to discourage her from ever getting back into the fast lane, there were signs in her career, too. Only one commitment had interrupted the transition to life in Ireland, and it can be looked upon as a minor theatrical disaster.

The show was *Prettybelle,* a Bob (*Funny Girl*) Merrill musical that seemed to have everything going for it. Jule Styne was the composer, and Gower Champion was to direct. And the title character, Prettybelle Sweet, was a middle-aged eccentric with a heart of gold, very much like Mame. What could go wrong?

Apparently, just about everything. Angela had found the script for *Prettybelle* waiting for her when she came back from Bavaria following *Something For Everyone*. She'd jumped at it. Then came Anthony's drug crisis and the fire. But Angela had signed for *Prettybelle* and she would not go back on her word. This didn't prevent her, however, from having second and third thoughts about it.

Prettybelle tried to get a serious message across in musical comedy form, always a risky formula when aimed at an audience that wants entertainment, not ideology. In a small southern town, the sheriff's widow attempts to make amends for her husband's bigotry by offering her sexual charms to minority groups. The resultant uproar among the town's upright citizenry makes a good one-liner, but it can't hold an entire show together. Angela should have remembered from *Anyone Can Whistle* that such radical themes seldom make it to Broadway. Maybe she did, because she pestered the show's principals throughout rehearsals and the Boston run.

"I told Bob Merrill that the writing was topical, funny and touching, but it needed a whole point of view," she says. "And it all fell into the wrong hands. I told them they were wrong. Jule Styne is an incredible composer, but not the right person to write this score. Gower Champion, again, is not a book musical man."

Her instincts were right on target there. In his book *Broadway Musicals*, drama critic Martin Gottfried says this about Champion, "First a Broadway dancer, he'd gone on to stage such forties revues as *Small Wonder* and *Lend An Ear*. But Champion made his name in Hollywood, as a performer in film musicals. He seemed movie people rather than show people, and his early work reflected that."

Gower Champion's other credits up to that point had consisted entirely of non-book musicals like *Bye, Bye Birdie, Carnival, Hello, Dolly!* and *I Do, I Do!*—musicals in which the staging outweighed the script. He was out of his depth with *Prettybelle,* and the production showed it.

The show went into rehearsals right after Christmas, 1970,

opened at the Shubert Theater in Boston on February 1, 1971, and closed March 3. Angela, possibly remembering the bad press she'd gotten during *Dear World*, backed down on her demands for changes that might have saved the show. And, as with *Dear World*, when the show flopped she shouldered the responsibility for it.

"I compromised on *Prettybelle* and I have only myself to blame. I should have pulled out. It was a complete and utter fiasco. The score was nil. My performance was awful. It was a tragedy of good intentions."

Good intentions couldn't save the only other offer she had that year, a musical called *Sister*, based on the life of evangelist Aimee Semple MacPherson, that her brother Edgar was to have coproduced. The show couldn't get backers, and Angela saw this as the handwriting on the wall. It was yet another push in the direction of never working again. She flew back to Ireland without a backward glance. If it lasted the rest of her life or only until the day after tomorrow, this was the life she had chosen.

"I was on my way to becoming a very fat cook and gardener," she recalls with that unvarnished self-assesssment of hers. "Of course, it was an unrealistic and childlike desire on my part."

Nevertheless, she took the peace and tranquility of the uncomplicated Irish lifestyle while it was offered to her. And she had gotten her children back, healthy and whole again. Nothing else mattered.

Deirdre, in time, became a successful model and painter. Anthony would eventually study acting and composition at the Webber-Douglas School for Drama in London, the same school his mother had attended. The past was behind them, and Angela wanted to make certain it stayed that way.

When reporters questioned her about her children's emotional problems over the years, she gave them rote responses and then changed the subject, protecting her children's privacy. It wasn't until 1985, in a television interview with Barbara Walters, that she broke down on camera and told the complete story for the first time. What made the moment particularly touching was that in another part of the interview she had talked about the many masks actors must wear. How many masks had she had to wear in order to save her children!

Thousands of parents nationwide empathized with Angela that night. She gave them hope. That was why she had decided to "go public." She had been working with AWIC, Abused Wives in Crisis, and a number of drug rehabilitation programs for years. She would do whatever she could, including revealing her own anguish, in order to save others from this disease that had almost robbed her of her children.

The crisis is long over now, and Angela intends to keep it that way. Today nosy reporters are deflected with an icy politeness.

"I'm sorry," Angela will say with that steel-blue look that has worked so well for her on stage and screen. "It's a closed topic."

The Shaws' Irish parsonage became a spiritual home for others, too. It was understood that friends who were "just passing through" could count on being put up for as long as they wanted to stay. Fritz Holt, a long-time friend who was to coproduce the revival of *Gypsy* that would bring Angela back into the spotlight with a splash, recalls his stay.

"One morning I'm fast asleep in the guest room and there's this knock on the door. This lady sets down a tray with juice and coffee, stokes the coals of the little fireplace, then exits without a word. I come out of my grogginess and realize 'Gee, that was Angela!' She's like the mother of us all."

Another old friend, actress Jane Connell, who played Agnes Gooch to Angela's Mame and the Madwoman of Montmartre to her Madwoman of Chaillot, has this to say:

"Angela is really very domestic. At times she'll be working and get wistful, saying 'I should be at home with my roses.' She loves to garden, and whenever she's performing there has to be a good kitchen at hand where she can cook."

For two years about all she did was garden and cook, recharge her batteries and wait with typical Libran patience to see what would turn up next. Once again, it was Peter who sensed when the time was right, then prodded Angela back into the public arena.

"I was terribly afraid," she admits. "But I agreed and started with timid baby steps. I knew the kids would be going their separate ways soon. I went over to London—you could fly there cheap from Cork; it was like taking a bus—and talked the Royal Shakespeare Company into letting me do Edward Albee's play *All Over*. That was perfect for me because the play was in repertory with two others, which meant that I could be in Ireland with the family and fly over for just three performances a week."

If only one could have been the proverbial fly on the wall during that conversation. Not everyone could convince the distinguished Royal Shakespeare to give her such a plum role. But the appeal of this multi-talented lady must have been irresistible. She was proven "box office." And her powers of persuasion had not lessened since she bounced into Albert Lewin's office at Metro to win Sybil Vane away from far more experienced actresses. Whatever means she employed, Angela was cast as The Mistress in the Albee play. That was the icebreaker.

Gradually she began to stretch her wings. A limited regional tour of *Mame* seemed a good place to start. The sense of déjà vu must have been overwhelming.

"Spooky," is what Angela called it. "In life you seldom get a chance to see history repeat itself."

If she was worried that she might be playing it too safe, appearing in a retread of an old vehicle, she exercised as much creative control as possible to make sure that this revival of *Mame* wasn't an also-ran.

"This is not just another packaged summer stock show, you see," she made quite clear. "I agreed to do it only on the condition that I could have the featured performers who were on Broadway with me.

"Besides, it's all Zero Mostel's fault," she quipped, referring to Mostel's overwhelming success in *Fiddler On The Roof,* which he would parlay into a full time career for the rest of his life. Besides, if there was a fresh audience waiting for *Mame,* and she could do it, who was she to argue?

There were practical considerations as well. Paramount Pictures had just bought the movie rights to *Mame.* Logic suggested that no one had a better shot at the role than Angela. Still, it never hurt to hedge one's bets. If she could prove audiences still loved her onstage, wooing Paramount into giving her the part would be easy.

The tour opened at the Camden New Jersey Music Fair. If audiences heard a special poignancy in "If He Walked into My Life," they thought it was only Angela the professional pulling out the stops and giving them a great performance. They couldn't know the secret scars, the special triumph, the song would always represent for her.

Next it was on to the Shady Grove Music Fair in Washington, D.C., where the audience was top-heavy with political celebrities and, one night, Tricia Nixon Cox accompanied by a busload of Secret Service men.

This part of the tour had its lighter moments. When she developed a leg cramp during Mame's energetic high kicks one night, Angela found herself being treated backstage by the physician for the University of Washington's football team.

There were disappointments, too. Paramount had made up its mind. At one A.M., after a performance, Angela served omelets, white wine, and strawberries and cream to reporters in her nearby hotel-suite-with-kitchen, and talked about losing the film version of *Mame* to Lucille Ball.

"I'm disappointed," she admitted, dishing up bacon and salad and pouring more wine. "But Lucille Ball is a great talent."

She would continue to be gracious even when Lucille Ball was not. The outrageous redhead, never known for her subtlety, made some snide remarks to reporters about how Angela couldn't take the role because of trouble in the family. With extraordinary cattiness, Lucille Ball made specific reference to Anthony's "illness." Amazed and deeply hurt, Angela refused to play the game at Ball's level.

"I think she made those remarks out of a mistaken sense of kindness," she said coolly. "I don't blame Lucy a bit."

She did blame Paramount, or at least chide them for their lack of judgement.

"The same studio," she pointed out, "bought *My Fair Lady* and replaced Julie Andrews, because she wasn't a name, with Audrey Hepburn, who couldn't sing. Julie won an Oscar that year for *Mary Poppins*."

110

As far as Angela was concerned, it was just another example of her underestimation by movie moguls. She wound up her tour of *Mame* at the Westbury Music Fair on Long Island, and refused to let it get to her.

In a rare bit of poetic justice, Lucille Ball had a perfectly miserable time shooting *Mame*. She balked and bullied until she got her way with casting, insisting on Bea Arthur to recreate the role of Vera, and Robert Preston to play Beau. She threw tantrums that antagonized the entire crew, and while it may not be entirely true that if the grips hate you your career is over, Miss Ball emerged in the final cut looking rather peaked.

In addition, shooting had to be held up for several weeks, ostensibly because the star was "suffering from exhaustion." In truth she had lost her voice during a screaming fit at the costume mistress, and couldn't talk, much less sing, for over a week. And on top of everything else, the critics almost universally panned the film. By anyone's definition, it was a flop.

While Lucille Ball was busy making herself hated, Angela was remembering what it was like to be loved—by a Broadway audience. The spring of 1973 found her in New York for one glittering night, appearing in *Sondheim: A Musical Tribute*. Everyone who was anyone who had ever been involved in a Sondheim show or sung a Sondheim song was there. Angela was invited, along with Leonard Bernstein, Anthony Perkins, Jack Cassidy, Harold Prince, Burt Shevelove, Nancy Walker, and Stephen Sondheim himself, to contribute her remarks between musical numbers. She then joined original *Anyone Can Whistle* cast member Harvey Evans and others in singing "Anyone Can Whistle," "There Won't Be Trumpets," "Me and My Town" and "A Parade in Town."

It was a grandiose class reunion that filled the Shubert Theatre to capacity. It convinced Angela of one thing. She'd been bitten by the bug again. Despite her disclaimers about being a cabbage, about being content with her family and her roses, *this* was what her life was all about. There was no business like show business.

*I*t was her brother Edgar's idea to revive *Gypsy* and to star Angela as Rose, the character Ethel Merman had belted into musical history.

Edgar Lansbury had come far since he'd flopped as the Big Bad Wolf at the age of five. The producer of *The Subject Was Roses, The Alchemist, Arms And The Man*, and *To Be Young, Gifted And Black*, among others, had always wanted to produce a show starring his talented sister.

He had actually proposed the idea to Angela two years earlier. Angela had turned him down. To say that she had trepidations about the part was putting it mildly. After all, Ethel Merman *was* Mama Rose Lee. She had created the role in 1959 and sung it all over the world in her inimitable style, which Martin Gottfried described this way:

"She [Merman] brought out in a composer the reason he wrote for the theater in the first place. There was that voice, a physical thing, pushing out from the stage in ever wider, pulsating throbs. She didn't merely introduce 'I Get a Kick Out of You,' 'There's No Business Like Show Business' and 'Everything's Coming Up Roses,' she shoved them in our faces, and we loved it."

No one had ever accused Angela of having a voice or a style like that. If she was going to do the role, she would have to find a totally different approach.

She held out for two years. But Edgar and his producing partner Joe Beruh were relentless. *Gypsy* had never been done in London, they pointed out. Elaine Stritch, fresh from her big success in *Company,* was itching to do Rose, but backers were lukewarm about her. They would go for Angela, Edgar pointed out, and so would the audience. What was she afraid of?

Angela weighed the proposition in her Libran scales. It would be wonderful to have a hit in London, the city of her birth, but devastating to fail there. Rose, the archetypal stage mother who pushed and bullied her daughters onto the burlesque stage because she had been denied a career of her own, was an appealing character. It would be so easy to play her as a monster, such a challenge to play her as a feeling human being. Was Angela up to the challenge?

The whole key was in finding an interpretation so different from Ethel Merman's that audiences wouldn't even think of her. Was it really so difficult? Merman was all voice, pure musical bombast; she was by her own admission no actress. Angela, on the other hand, could assess her own talent this way:

"If I occupy any rear seat at all in the theater, it is primarily as an actress, not as a musical personality."

It was Walter Kerr who was to put into perspective the absolute difference between these two performers in the same role. In his *Journey To The Center Of The Theater,* the veteran *New York Times* drama critic and observer wrote, "Miss Lansbury is not really to be compared to Miss Merman: there's no way of doing it. Miss Merman is a natural force, like the Colorado River (I have never seen the Colorado River; I don't feel the need to, having seen Miss Merman). Miss Lansbury is half fine actress, half ferocious personality, admirable because she works so hard and, in working so hard, works so honestly. Divorce the two in your mind. The stars these stars were born under come from entirely different constellations."

Angela may not have been able to put the difference into such perfect words, but she knew the difference was there. And when

Gypsy writer Arthur Laurents, who had been a trusted friend since *Anyone Can Whistle,* asked her to read the script one more time, she felt her resolve weakening.

There was no question that, regardless of the title, *Gypsy* was Rose's show. How many times had Angela taken characters worse than Rose and found some truth and beauty in them? Could she do it again? She would have the support of Laurents' book and, once again, Stephen Sondheim's lyrics. If she refused for a niggling personal reason like cold feet, she would never forgive herself. Every time Angela looked at her, Rose was looking better and better.

"As a woman, I look for the fascinating facets and truths behind people that can make the worst bitch in the world a palatable human being," is how she puts it. *"Gypsy* is really about the tragedy of good intentions. Rose is a pathetic person, but her guts make her riveting, exciting, and extremely stage-worthy."

She was hooked. She told Laurents she had found the added depth she was looking for. She sat down with Edgar and Joe Beruh and signed for the length of the run. She admitted she was still "insecure," but she was going for it.

Gypsy would open in London in June, 1973. Following a limited run it would take off on a tour from Toronto to Los Angeles and across America, ending in New York over a year later. Angela was committed to her longest run since *Mame.* It was Rose's turn.

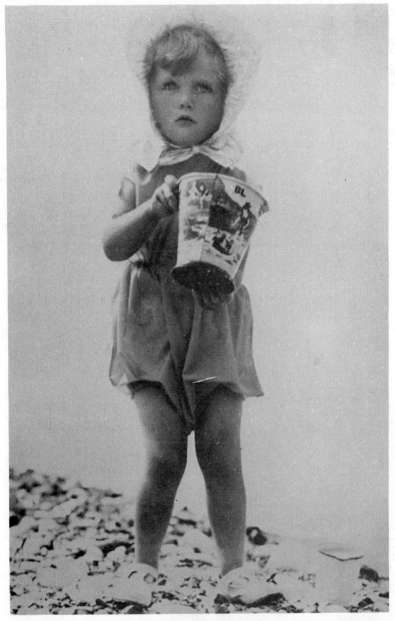

Angela Lansbury at the age of three at Birchington-on-Sea in Sussex.
(The Museum of Modern Art/Film Stills Archive)

"Pouty and pomaded," as Bosley Crowther described her in The Private Affairs of Bel Ami. *(The Museum of Modern Art/Film Stills Archive)*

As Sybil Vane in The Picture of Dorian Gray. *(The Museum of Modern Art/Film Stills Archive)*

*With first husband, Richard Cromwell. (*The Museum of Modern Art/Film Stills Archive)

*Angela with her twin brothers, Bruce and Edgar, circa 1945. (*The Museum of Modern Art/Film Stills Archive)

As the Philistine beauty Semader in Samson and Delilah. *(*The Museum of Modern Art/Film Stills Archive*)*

With Peter Shaw, on their wedding day, August 12, 1949. (The Museum of Modern Art/Film Stills Archive)

Mame: 1966. (Courtesy of the Billy Rose Collection of The New York Public Library at Lincoln Center)

As world-famous mystery writer, Jessica Fletcher. (Universal/Shooting Star)

On location for "Murder, She Wrote" with Ned Beatty, Arthur Hill, and Brian Keith. (Universal/Shooting Star)

With "Murder, She Wrote" sheriff Tom Bosley (left) and Claude Akins. (Universal/ Shooting Star)

Jessica Fletcher in Talbot's Cove, location of "Murder, She Wrote." (Universal/Shooting Star)

With cast members from "Murder, She Wrote." (Universal/Shooting Star)

Jessica contemplates a crime on "Murder, She Wrote." (Universal/Shooting Star)

> *Opening night was like a football game. People cheered through a fifteen-minute standing ovation, grown men cried unashamed, the backstage area looked like a flower shop on Mother's Day. Her homecoming in* Gypsy *is the most exciting thing since V-E Day.*
>
> —REX REED

*A*ll of London had something to talk about that night—their expatriate homecoming queen. She had left London thirty years before as a little girl with a dream. On June 9, 1973, she came back to the Piccadilly Theatre like gangbusters. Even so jaded a theater critic as the late Kenneth Tynan remarked, "In twenty years of London theatre, I've never seen anything like this."

Composer Jule Styne, Arthur Laurents, and Stephen Sondheim met her backstage. Their opinion was unanimous:

"We saw our show for the first time."

The audience had gone wild. During the fifteen-minute standing ovation, a voice from the balcony shouted: "Welcome home!"

"I had to forget all about Ethel Merman," was how Angela explained how she had found her own way to play the character. "I've heard her sing the songs countless times at parties, but I never saw the show, luckily, so I approached it just as I would any new role. I tried to find a core of honesty in the part, instead of playing a caricature of the stage mother."

Merman herself never managed to see Angela in the role, either in London or in the states, even though she was performing at the London Palladium and doing a concert in San Francisco while *Gypsy* was touring there. Nevertheless, she was diplomatic about Angela's doing "her" role.

"I wish her luck and I know she'll be great," Merman was quoted as saying. "I've no hard feelings. Why should I? I could have had the role if I wanted to. I'm just so glad I created the role so others can copy it."

The two stars had had a confrontation at a party shortly after Angela signed to do the role.

"I hear you're going to do *Gypsy*," Merman said, cutting to the heart of the matter.

"Nobody but you can do *Gypsy*," Angela replied. "But I'm going to have a go at it."

Have a go at it she did, in a way that had critics puzzling for years over exactly what it was she had done. They almost unanimously came to the conclusion that Angela had found an entirely new meaning to the character of Rose, and in so doing virtually created a new *Gypsy*.

"It is she who takes the insensitive, cruelly ambitious Rose and makes her first pitiful and then gallant," Martin Gottfried wrote in the *Post* when he saw the show in New York. "She who grasps the running theme of Rose's dreams and goes beyond them into near madness and the lady's ironclad heart. Miss Lansbury spearheads the show's brutality and then overcomes it with devastating compassion."

"I marveled at *Gypsy* the first time I saw it," Walter Kerr wrote. "And I marveled all over again in 1974 as I watched Angela Lansbury step not into Ethel Merman's shoes—Miss Merman's are sturdy, nailed into space, while Miss Lansbury's are feverishly elusive—but into those cobbled so craftily for Mama Rose, mother of Gypsy Rose Lee and 'Baby June' Havoc, self-sacrificing tigress, secret seeker of the spotlight, a creature demonic and doting in each savage embrace."

Angela took a much less poetic view of what she had done.

"I have two audiences, actually—the people who love to see me play bitches and the ones who want to see me sing and dance—and

116

this role has everything so it's perfect for me," she said, making it sound easy.

It was not easy, of course, not by any means. In terms of sheer stamina the role could have killed a horse.

"I'm on the stage almost every minute like a pile driver," Angela confided to columnist Earl Wilson. "One thing God gave me was energy. I really do an eleven o'clock number at 7:45 and another eleven o'clock number at the end of the show."

Still, there she was the morning after the London opening, wading through stacks of newspapers full of excellent reviews, scuffing around in slippers, ironing, sending wires to actor friends opening in other shows. She could transform the rented flat into home with nothing more than a freshly brewed pot of tea and her own homey magic. Son Anthony and a pack of his guitar-playing friends lolled around in the clutter eating cream cheese sandwiches Angela had made for them as if she were just anyone's doting Mum.

She had also managed to find her son gainful employment, as dialogue coach for *Gypsy*. Having grown up surrounded by transatlantic accents, Anthony was good at helping the British members of the company polish their American accents.

"Mum got me a job in the production company," Anthony, who is now dialogue coach for "Murder, She Wrote," remembers.

From there everything began to fall into place for the young man. "It gave me enough of a sense of self-worth that I entered drama school and took myself to a very fine psychiatrist who put the finishing touches on cleaning me up from the drugs. I ended up doing good work as an actor in British television and films."

With her private life in order, Angela and her pile driver wowed London for seven months. Then it was on the road for another seven. From Toronto to nightly sellouts at the Shubert Theater in Los Angeles, from Westbury, Long Island to Valley Forge, from Dallas to Oklahoma, Angela and *Gypsy* won all their hearts. She came to love the character as much as the people watching her. Rose had become as much a part of her soul as Mame.

"You lose your identity in these musicals. They allow you to be-

117

come the character you're playing. You like yourself better after the performance."

Rave reviews followed her wherever she went.

"If she [Angela] seemed at first glance to be too young and beautiful to be believable," Martin Gottfried wrote, "her thoughtful acting and stylish, energetic rendering of the songs quickly won over skeptics. *Gypsy* delighted again."

The tour closed with a limited engagement in New York, only because Angela's doctor was convinced she'd run herself into the ground. At one point she did manage to strain her voice severely enough to warrant complete rest for forty-eight hours; Rose is notoriously one of the worst roles for throats. Angela's response to being told not to utter a sound for two whole days was:

"It's hard to keep my mouth shut."

Strange things began to happen to her as opening night on Broadway drew closer. If standing in Ethel Merman's shadow wasn't intimidating enough, being in the first play to open the 1974 Broadway season certainly was. Then there were the block-long signs covering the marquee in front of the Winter Garden with big red letters that shouted "Angela Lansbury in *Gypsy*" and "Here She Is, Boys . . . Here She Is, World . . . Here's Angela!" The center of all this attention began to develop sniffles, hives, and a number of other ailments.

"Broadway is still the challenge," she explains. "I'd been healthy as a horse until we got there. Then all these psychosomatic illnesses, the throat, and I blew up like a balloon. In Boston I was a basket case.

"When we opened at the Winter Garden, I wasn't myself at all. I had a bad cold. I felt sicker than that, really, because I knew in New York I'd be compared with Ethel Merman and I wanted to be at my best."

She had nothing to fear. *New York Times* columnist John Corry recorded the big moment this way:

"The curtain fell, and then it rose, and the members of the company came out taking bows and being applauded. Angela Lansbury, however, came out alone, the way a big Broadway star does, and when she did the applause became louder. It was louder than it had been in Dallas, Los Angeles, or even London. Broadway, after all, is something else."

Angela agreed.

"Broadway always is and always has been the place where you had to make it—the last pin you had to knock down."

She was enormously grateful for the audience's reception, but still skeptical about whether or not she had "made it."

"The warmth of the audience—that doesn't mean a damn thing," explained the star who had had audiences eating out of her hand in *Anyone Can Whistle*. "It's difficult to continue in a show unless you have the critics. They're what count."

Not that she had to worry about the critics this time out. Following the traditional appearance at Sardi's after the opening, the cast was invited to a lavish backers' party at the Tower Suite. As part of the opening night ritual, one of the producers grabbed a microphone and proceeded to read the first review, hot off the presses.

"It was a rotten microphone, by the way," Angela the perfectionist remembers. "But it was a good review. Then I knew we were halfway there."

With that reassurance, she and Peter left the party early, retiring to their hotel suite overlooking the Museum of Modern Art to have their own private celebration with a bottle of Paddy's Irish whiskey and a loaf of soda bread. New York's night life had welcomed them, but they would take it on their own terms.

"I have this incredible affection for New York," Angela says with a note of sadness in her voice. She is always sad to find that something is not as she remembers it. "But over the years I've watched it become a fortress. Even Broadway is becoming a no-no, with the buses bringing the poor dears in from the suburbs, and then picking them up and taking them home again. Still, I love the character of the city."

Not all her nights were spent in her hotel suite; between shows she managed to make the round of New York parties, dressing up then because she still tended to dress down for the everyday. Her philosophy that clothes are worn primarily to keep warm had not altered since she was a young starlet. The transformation when she did dress up, glittering with the blue sapphires she favored to accentuate the blue of her eyes, was always extraordinary. She could walk around in an old sweater and slacks all day, then turn up for a dinner hosted by Rex Reed at the chic restaurant Katja's wearing a sable coat over a clingy Scott Barrie original.

Generally speaking, however, she preferred quiet dinners with friends, with an emphasis on good food and good conversation. Old friends know she will tolerate neither late-comers nor people who monopolize the conversation. Ever the gracious hostess, she expects her guests to be equally gracious.

The short New York run turned out to be a blessing. Her family needed Angela's attention. Peter had recently had hip surgery to cure a pre-arthritic condition, and Angela was able to nurse him during his recuperation. And her mother soon needed her desperately.

Well into her seventies, the once-beautiful Moyna MacGill had suffered some serious health problems since her retirement. A broken hip kept her bedridden for months. She developed throat cancer and a laryngectomy bought her some time against this disfiguring killer disease, but at great cost. The lovely Irish actress whose lyric voice had charmed theater and movie audiences on two continents was robbed of the power of speech by the devastating surgery.

But if Angela was no quitter, it was because Moyna had taught her how. With her daughter's help over the last summer of her life, Moyna relearned how to speak. Without vocal chords, she fought to communicate through esophageal speech, a special breathing technique that uses surviving parts of the esophagus to reproduce sound.

Moyna had taught Angela to sing and dance and mimic British comediennes when she was a little girl. She had struggled and scrimped so that her talented child could have every opportunity to succeed in show business, then stepped back quietly into her own modest career while that child became a star.

Now the roles were reversed, and it was Angela who taught her mother how to speak, nurturing her along like a child, endlessly patient. If she was aware of the irony of this role reversal, she kept her feelings to herself. She was too busy making Moyna's last months meaningful, and hiding her own sorrow. It was the least she could do for the mother who had taught her everything she knew.

Moyna MacGill died in the autumn of 1975. She had wanted to be cremated, and Angela took care of the final arrangements. She had Moyna's ashes scattered in the heather in a peaceful green valley close by the old Irish vicarage. Angela had brought her mother home.

Fifteen weeks after its New York opening, *Gypsy* closed on January 4, 1975, though not before paying off its backers in time for Christmas. Angela was gratified that the many small investors got their money back.

"These are people with little stakes, actors and dressers and everybody."

Gypsy had been familiar territory for over a year and a half; it was not going to be easy to let it go.

"I could cry when I think of not doing it anymore," Angela told columnist Earl Wilson on the day after Christmas, 1974. Still, as she pointed out, she had managed to find her own voice, without in any way infringing on Ethel Merman's creation. "Her approach to it was so pristine and perfect that there was no reason for anybody to compare us."

And when she received her third Tony Award for *Gypsy,* Angela acknowledged Merman in her acceptance speech.

"Well, I thought it was her due. She created this lady in the first place and received no recognition except from the audiences."

Ethel Merman, in return, wrote Angela a gracious letter of thanks, which Angela received while tending to her mother in Ireland. The new Tony had by then joined its two elder sisters on the mantle of the big fireplace in the parlor. It was a fitting reward for what had been one of the most satisfying experiences of her creative life.

The reason I was able to segue from movies into musical theater? I think most good tragedians are also good comedians. To be really tragic, you also have to be a clown.

T he mid-seventies were a mixed bag for Angela. Coming down from the long, exhausting run of *Gypsy,* she didn't want to commit herself to anything else long-term right away. There was the pull of the Irish lifestyle again, reminding her to take time to smell the roses and, when necessary, go after them with the pruning shears. Both Anthony and Deirdre had left the nest, and Angela and Peter had some time to themselves. But one little offer was about to lure Angela away before too long. All it needed was a quick commute to London.

There probably isn't an actor in the English-speaking world who can turn down Shakespeare. Angela had simply never been offered the opportunity. The Old Vic was in the process of mounting a production of *Hamlet,* with Albert Finney in the title role. Director Peter Hall invited Angela to play Gertrude.

During the seventies, productions of *Hamlet* increasingly stressed the possibility of an incestuous relationship between the tormented Hamlet and his too-lusty-for-her-own-good mother. The Old Vic production did not resort to such blatancy, but played the Bard straight.

"I must say sex never reared its head, disappointing some," Angela recalls.

With her usual cool professionalism, she dismissed any qualms or stage nerves she may have had about approaching Shakespeare for the very first time and in such distinguished company at this point in her life. She would play Gertrude with as much heart and dedication to detail as she had any other stage role in her long and varied career.

"I paid my dramatic dues. That was simply my first real lunge at Shakespeare."

If she had little else to say about the experience, it may have been because on the whole it was rather disappointing. Maybe her expectations had been too great. Maybe she found the restrictions of Shakespearean dialogue stifling. But she wasn't about to commit the artistic gaffe of criticizing Shakespeare. It would be years before she admitted that she thought the Bard just wasn't what he was cracked up to be. She expressed this unorthodox opinion during the run of *Sweeney Todd*, whose Mrs. Lovett was about as far removed from Gertrude as one could get.

"I find it very trying playing restrained roles," was how she put it. "I had a nice quiet role playing Gertrude in *Hamlet* a couple of years ago in London and I hated it."

One can imagine Shakespeare turning in his grave, but chuckling a little at the same time. He would have admired Angela for her honesty.

Angela probably should have counted her blessings. The year after her lunge at Shakespeare would find her fluttering back to New York to occupy herself with some less-than-classical things.

There was her singing the "Star Spangled Banner" in Central Park in June as part of the American Bicentennial celebration. It was a pleasant enough patriotic gesture for her adopted country, but only one of the far too many celebrity appearances that were part of the general hooplah. There was the voice-over for a Christmas cartoon so memorable it is not even listed in her credits. And there was *The 1976 Milliken Breakfast Show.*

Maybe it was just the urge to show her fans she could still do those high kicks with the best of them. But there she was at 7 A.M. every weekday morning for the entire month of June, in the grand ballroom of the Waldorf-Astoria Hotel, costarring with Robert

Morse, Georgia Engel and a forty-eight-member chorus line, singing the praises of Deering, Milliken yarns and fabrics to an audience of up to two thousand clothing retailers and fashion buyers.

Under the headline "Angela Lansbury Selling Sweaters," *The Wall Street Journal* critiqued this parody of *A Chorus Line,* with songs like "If You Knew Sportswear Like I Know Sportswear" (to the tune of "If You Knew Susie . . .") as being a great good time.

"It is novel and fun to see stars of the magnitude of Miss Lansbury and Mr. Morse taking a fling at something like this."

These so-called "industrial" shows have a reputation for being shoddily produced and generally second-rate, too concerned with hawking merchandise to pay attention to artistic detail. But with its one and one-half million dollar annual budget and well-choreographed casts of up to seventy performers, *The Milliken Breakfast Show* was considered the best of the lot. Certainly it was the most expensive. And anything that gave Angela a chance to kick up her heels could make even a jaded, sleepy audience love her.

Between long runs in Broadway musicals, Angela had always managed to find roles to stretch her. The year after the Milliken extravaganza, she hung up her dancing shoes and took on a pair of serious, contained roles in a double-header by Edward Albee.

Her experience with Albee's unique style of dramatic writing had begun earlier with *All Over* at the Royal Shakespeare. She was now invited to perform in *Counting The Ways* and *Listening,* two Albee one-acts featured in repertory at the Hartford Stage Company.

Asked to describe the two plays, Albee characterized them both as "examining the breakdown in communication in society and among individuals." That this could apply to *any* Albee play indicates how difficult it is for an actor to get a handle on these tenuous conceptual dramas, much less give life and credibility to a character within such a vehicle.

Angela was going to try. *Counting The Ways* had premiered the year before at Britain's National Theatre with Beryl Reid in the role she was now to play. She was to costar with the distinguished Broadway veteran William Prince and the gifted Maureen Anderman. Albee himself was to direct.

Albee described *Counting The Ways* as "a series of vaudeville black-outs involving husband and wife." *Listening* was characterized only as "a chamber piece, musical in form, with recurring themes and arias." Both plays were small cast, intimate domestic dramas, bred out of the unique hothouse environment Albee knows and writes of with familiarity.

For someone who professed to dislike restrained roles, Angela was challenging herself yet again. The two plays ran in repertory with such contemporary classics as *Waltz Of The Toreadors* and *The Glass Menagerie* from January into March, 1976.

Two films were to follow at a leisurely pace over the next year. The first, *Death On The Nile,* was an attempt to catch the coattails of the Agatha Christie mania born again with the release of *Murder On The Orient Express.* The second, *The Lady Vanishes,* was a grossly inferior remake of the old Margaret Rutherford classic. Neither was memorable, neither did anything at all for Angela, except act as a kind of foreshadowing for her role in "Murder, She Wrote."

Death On The Nile, shot in London and on location in Egypt, starred Peter Ustinov as Miss Christie's legendary detective, Hercule Poirot. Like its predecessor, *Murder On The Orient Express,* it featured a star-studded cast, which included Bette Davis, Mia Farrow, David Niven, Olivia Hussey, Jack Warden, Maggie Smith, and of course Angela. The plot was the typical exotic-locale Christie brain twister about an heiress murdered on a steamer cruising down the Nile, and the indefatigable Hercule Poirot being called in to unravel the mystery. The result was not even high camp.

"This new Agatha Christie movie," wrote Hilton Kramer in the *New York Times,* "is a big, expensive, star-studded bore in which a lot of famous talent is permitted—no, encouraged—to do a series of campy turns on their own worst mannerisms."

In *Murder On The Orient Express,* Albert Finney had played Poirot. His interpretation was extremely high camp, but he managed to walk a careful tightrope between subtlety and travesty. Peter Ustinov, apparently, fell off the wire.

"Whether he is parodying Agatha Christie or only himself would be difficult to say," Hilton Kramer wrote of Angela's former brother-in-law. He had equally unkind things to say about the rest of the cast, praising the costumer and the makeup man for the only significant contributions to the fiasco. Angela, for her part, at least got a chance to travel to a part of the world she'd never seen before.

The Lady Vanishes didn't do even that much for her. She'd already been to Bavaria with *Something For Everyone*. And *The Lady Vanishes* was the kind of experience that would have made a lesser actress throw movies over altogether.

Blame the direction, blame the trend in casting that makes it possible for football players, models and the like to become actors overnight without benefit of talent or training. The original *Lady Vanishes*, with frumpy old Margaret Rutherford in the title role, was a tightly constructed Alfred Hitchcock classic, the kind of grainy black and white beauty with which to while away a rainy Sunday afternoon or sit up with a bowl of popcorn at 3 A.M. to catch on the late movie. The greatness of these old films is that they hold up through endless re-viewings. Knowing "how it turns out" is not nearly as important as following the process through again and again, marveling at its seamlessness.

The remake of *The Lady Vanishes*, which had as its only advantage Angela's re-interpretation of Miss Froy, does not even hold up under one viewing. Whatever Cybill Shepherd and Elliott Gould are doing on that screen, it is not acting. Mr. Gould is as usual playing Elliott Gould, a character with which he is obviously familiar, but whose portrayal leaves the audience with a big "Who cares?" Cybill Shepherd's hand-flapping gee-whiz high school drama club portrayal is an embarrassment. Leslie Halliwell's comment that the remake was "not even a fair copy" of the original is simply too kind.

Angela can be forgiven for accepting the role for several reasons. First, *Lady* was the middle of a package of three films in the murder mystery genre she had signed to do; *The Mirror Crack'd* was to be the third. Secondly, she was trying to do something different with Miss Froy. Just as she had refused to copy Ethel Merman's Rose in *Gypsy*, but examined the role from all sides to find a way that she could do it and make it fresh, she refused to copy Margaret Rutherford's En-

126

glish sheepdog interpretation of Miss Froy. Angela's Miss Froy is a dapper, tweedy proper English lady with a hint of the risqué and a perfect ability to take care of herself, thank you, Nazi machine-guns notwithstanding. Angela found her own truth in Miss Froy, and played her as if she had never been played before. On that level she was successful.

And, lastly, she can hardly be blamed for the obvious lack of talent or discipline evidenced by her costars. In fact, Ms. Shepherd and Mr. Gould might have been grateful that in more than one instance she saved their shared scenes from utter hopelessness.

Nevertheless, it must have been a relief to have both films done and an interesting fling in theater to look forward to. Angela had been signed as Constance Towers' summer replacement in *The King And I* while Miss Towers took a much needed three-week vacation from the Broadway smash. For a mere twenty-four performances, Angela was to play Anna to the King of Siam. It was a three-week run that was to set the critical community leaping out of its house seats right on its ear.

"*I* really don't think of my performance as a replacement," Angela told reporters when she stepped in for Constance Towers in *The King And I.* "It's simply a chance for me to get off my behind and do the sort of part that isn't written for women any more, not to mention having Richard Rodgers as your vocal coach."

Not to mention having to go through the entire rehearsal process in double time and stepping into a role for a mere three weeks. As Angela described it, she was just "keeping the part warm" until Constance Towers came back.

Producer Lee Guber, an old friend, had asked her to step in. It was an awful lot of work for an awfully short run in a borrowed role. Most other actresses would have turned it down. Angela couldn't resist.

For one thing, she had just signed to do Stephen Sondheim's controversial *Sweeney Todd.* What better way to get her feet wet, sound out the Broadway audience and see if they still loved her, than to pop into a ready-made role?

There was also the knowledge that Rodgers' and Hammerstein's "Mrs. Anna" was as close to an operatic role as could be written for a musical; for someone who had always been put down by Hollywood for her "reedy little voice," the role offered a chance to show what she was really made of.

And, as she had pointed out, not everyone had the honor of having Richard Rodgers for her personal vocal coach. Rodgers worked with Angela on the score, returning to the original libretto he had written for the show's original star, Gertrude Lawrence. It was a wise move. In terms of talent and acting style, Angela was far closer to Gertrude Lawrence than to anyone else who had done Mrs. Anna.

Interestingly enough, *The King And I* had been written as a star vehicle for Gertrude Lawrence. The role of the king was considered a "supporting lead," i.e. a secondary role. When Yul Brynner was first cast, he was a virtually unknown film actor with only three credits for supporting roles on Broadway. But when Gertrude Lawrence died in the middle of the original three-year run, Brynner's energy and natural magnetism changed the focus of the play. From then on it was the king's show.

But for Angela's three-week run, Yul Brynner would also be on vacation. Michael Kermoyan, who ordinarily played the Kralahome, the Chief Minister, and who had frequently filled in for Brynner, would be taking over the role at the same time Angela did. Would this change the dynamics of the show? No one would know until the first performance.

Richard Rodgers instinctively coached Angela using the libretto he had written for Gertrude Lawrence. Some songs and dances were slightly restaged, some new Irene Sharoff costumes provided, but otherwise no special accommodations were made for Angela. It was assumed the old pro didn't need them.

"The odd thing," Rex Reed wrote, "is that everyone expected her to be perfect, forgetting that she had to learn all that dialogue, work her way into costume fittings, assume a characterization and memorize the complicated blocking, without much rehearsal and without the benefit of one public preview. Lansbury gave them perfection, made it seem as natural as a waltz. She deserves a medal of honor."

Curiously, until she was asked to play Mrs. Anna, Angela had never seen a performance of *The King And I*.

"I never saw Gertrude Lawrence play Anna, and I don't understand why," she says. "Peter and I flew in frequently from the coast to catch the Broadway shows."

But like her never having seen Ethel Merman in *Gypsy*, this worked to her advantage. She had no preconceived notions of Lawrence's performance. She did, however, catch a performance with Constance Towers and Yul Brynner just before she began her own rehearsals, primarily to learn the blocking. She found herself as emotionally touched as the rest of the audience.

"I sat at a matinee and watched Yul and Constance move that huge audience to laughter and tears," she remembers. "We are emotional. We need to laugh and cry in a theater."

Now it was her turn to see if she could make an audience do the same. She was excited at the prospect of doing some "legitimate singing. Suddenly I'm doing it on the level. No one wants to dub me now. Although it has taken me awhile, I feel that I've gotten my own back.

"I came to New York this winter to explore new possibilities and to look for a way to get my Broadway legs back for next season," she explained, referring to the upcoming *Sweeney Todd*.

For the moment at least, those Broadway legs were hidden in hoopskirts. Even so, Angela knocked 'em dead yet again.

"Lansbury looks, sounds and is enchanting as Anna," the *Daily News* hailed her, referring to her run in *King* as "the shortest stardom in Rodgers and Hammerstein history."

In the *New York Post,* Clive Barnes gave serious analysis to what Angela had done. Under the headline "THE KING AND NEW 'I'," he praised Michael Kermoyan's performance as "just fine," and went on to say, "The role of Anna was written for an intelligent voice rather than a great voice, and Miss Lansbury points up the drama of every song with unobtrusive delicacy, capturing the no-nonsense Englishness of this extremely Anglo-Saxon school marm."

Rex Reed abandoned analysis for ecstatic praise. It was he who had quoted Angela as wanting to "just keep the role warm" until Constance Towers returned.

"All good intentions aside," Reed wrote, "Lansbury made it evident Tuesday night that she's not only keeping the role warm, she's sending it up in flames. Gertrude Lawrence was charming, but she couldn't sing for beans. And while Constance Towers sings beautifully, she can't touch Lansbury as an actress."

Review after review waxed poetic about Angela in *The King And I*, and there seemed to be some sort of movement afoot to nominate her as "First Lady of the Musical Theater." The usually staid *New York Times* actually went so far as to suggest it in print. And the *Daily News* pointed out:

"In the past dozen years, Lansbury has become one of Broadway's most valued musical stars, with a quality all her own. And along with her charming presence and skill as an actress, she has a singing voice capable of floating all those lovely songs Rodgers and Hammerstein wrote for Anna most agreeably."

And Clive Barnes remarked, "Miss Lansbury is an actress first and a singer second. She also understands precisely what musical comedy acting is all about—its diagrammatic exaggeration, its emblematic gestures, its sense of heightened naturalism."

Angela must have been terribly pleased. She had always characterized herself as an actress who could sing. Now the critics at last understood and agreed with her.

All this praise must have been heady, and perhaps a little frightening. Still, it proved one thing. Broadway was ready for her once again, even in something as offbeat and bizarre as *Sweeney Todd* would prove to be.

With that Cupid's-bow mouth set in that strong-chinned face, she has always had a beguiling mixture of toughness and sex appeal, and time and again it is her performance one has carried away.

—MICHAEL BILLINGTON,
The New York Times

Theater is strenuous. You have to pace yourself, learn to give the audience the illusion of an all-stops-pulled-out performance.

The illusion began again in September of 1978, with the first rehearsal of *Sweeney Todd*. Armed with a rolling pin and a greasy apron, Angela was about to give life to one of the zaniest characters ever to tread the Broadway boards—Mrs. Nellie Lovett, baker of nineteenth-century London's most unusual pies.

"I think it's going to be a Grand Guignol," Angela explained when she was first enticed into doing Sondheim's latest creation. "Something we haven't seen on Broadway in a long time. Our show will be horrendous—the blackest comedy. Remember the movie *The Lodger*? Remember the atmosphere, the look, the fabric? That's what this is supposed to be. At the same time, you're supposed to scream with laughter. And God help us if it's not there."

She was referring to a style of theater, originating in France, featuring tales of the gruesome or horrible. *Sweeney Todd* was certainly to be both. Its story, based on a Victorian legend, had been dramatically presented during the nineteenth century, and a contemporary

132

version by Christopher Bond entitled *Sweeney Todd, The Demon Barber Of Fleet Street*, had been running at the Stratford East Theatre outside of London for two years. In collaboration with book writer Hugh Wheeler, Stephen Sondheim would create a near-opera.

It was a message play—about greed, injustice, and revenge—with the somewhat Brechtian suggestion that we are all secret murderers in our hearts. The message itself was a bit much for Broadway audiences to swallow. Worse, they tended to drown in the gore.

Benjamin Barker, so the legend goes, was a barber, an upstanding man with a beautiful wife. A lecherous judge lusted after the wife, and when she would not be untrue to her husband, had the hapless Mr. Barker falsely accused of a crime and exiled to Australia. Returning to London, the barber assumes the name of Sweeney Todd and seeks revenge on all who plotted with the judge against him, slitting their throats with missionary fervor and, with the help of Mrs. Lovett, transforming them into meat pies.

Harold Prince was to direct this larger-than-life *Sweeney Todd*, with Len Cariou in the title role. Prince and Sondheim wanted Angela for Mrs. Lovett.

Angela was indecisive at first. Her instincts about what would or would not play to a Broadway audience were finely honed by now; she had serious reservations about *Sweeney Todd*.

"I sensed this was controversial entertainment," she remembers. "A lot of people found the blood abhorrent. I wanted to see how the part [Mrs. Lovett] would shape up. It had to be commensurate with the Sweeney Todd character. I didn't want to hang around like a terrier doing nothing."

Once again it was husband Peter who did the convincing. He had been one of William Morris's top agents for good reason. He smelled a winner in *Sweeney Todd*, and talked Angela into it.

A strong selling point was costar Len Cariou. This magnificent actor had nearly twenty Broadway credits. He had done everything from Lear to Oedipus to Henry V to Orestes. Like Angela, he was an actor first and a singer second. He had starred opposite Lauren Bacall in *Applause*, and had won a Tony for *A Little Night Music*, another Sondheim show. He and Angela were to create a wonderful dynamism together.

They would have to. They had to hold their own against the set, a massive sixty-foot iron foundry (restructured by designer Eugene Lee and transported piecemeal to the stage of the Uris Theater), where it overhung the first six rows of orchestra seats, and against the more than two hours of Sondheim's almost continuous music, and relentless lyrics.

"It's Sondheim at his most," Angela reported during rehearsals. "I sing in voices I never used before, I belt in ranges I never belted in before. Len and I do a duet, he sings about one thing and me about something else, and we sing together. I also spend a good deal of time running, rather like the Keystone Kops."

Considering her dislike of restrained roles like Gertrude in *Hamlet* ("Mrs. Anna was a very restrained role, too," in her opinion), it probably served her right. From her opening number, where she admits to baking "The Worst Pies in London," to the final curtain where, rolling pin held triumphantly aloft, she takes her final bow, Mrs. Lovett is a workout. But what fun!

The fun became serious when, during previews, a near-deadly accident onstage showed the kind of stuff professional actors are made of. To understand the magnitude of the accident, it is necessary to comprehend the size of Eugene Lee's set. Richard Eder, writing in the *New York Times,* described it quite accurately.

"The set, a great contraption like a foundry with iron beams, moving bridges, and clanking wheels and belts, is grim and exuberant at the same time. When a back panel, a festering mass of rusty corrugated iron, lifts, a doleful scene of industrial London is exposed."

Three days from opening night, some of that rusting hulk apparently rusted through. Angela and Len Cariou were in the middle of the song "Not While I'm Around." Angela had just taken Cariou's arm to lead him downstage, singing the line "Nothing can harm you." It was to prove incredibly ironic. At that instant, one of the massive overhead bridges gave way and crashed to the stage only inches from where they had been standing.

134

As the echoes died away, everyone froze. The stage manager leaped onstage and stopped the show. Onstage, backstage and in the preview audience, no one dared move.

It was Angela who saved the day. With that incredible take-charge cool that is her trademark, she took a deep breath and went on with the song. She was greeted with scattered applause. Len Cariou shouted, "Everybody! Take Two!" and the show went on.

"The musical and dramatic achievements of Stephen Sondheim's black and bloody *Sweeney Todd* are so numerous and so clamorous that they trample and jam each other in that invisible but finite doorway that connects a stage and its audience, doing themselves some harm in the process," wrote Richard Eder on the opening. "There is more of artistic energy, creative personality and plain excitement in *Sweeney Todd,* which opened last night at the enormous Uris Theater and made it seem like a cottage, than in a dozen average musicals."

Giving points to the cast for sheer stamina in holding their own against what he called this "glittering, dangerous weapon" of a play, Mr. Eder singled out Len Cariou for transcending the straitjacket of his role.

"Mr. Cariou is to some degree a prisoner of his anguish; he slits throats with lordly abstraction but his role as deranged visionary doesn't give him much variety. He is such a strong actor, and such a fine singer, though, that he makes up for it with a kind of glow."

Turning his attention to Angela, the *Times* critic acknowledged her performance with a critique of equal impact.

"Her songs, many of them rapid patter songs with awkward musical intervals, and having to be sung while doing five or ten other things at once, are awesomely difficult and she does them awesomely well," he raved, waxing poetic. "Her voice is a visible voice; you can follow it amid any confusion; it is not piercing but piping. Her face is a comic face; her eyes revolve three times around to announce the arrival of an idea, but there is a blue sadness blinking behind them."

She could ask for no higher accolade. The weeks of "woodshedding," as she called it—trooping around Central Park in the New York winter with a tape recorder, drumming the lines into her head—had paid off. A lifetime of simply hanging in like a terrier until the right roles came along had rewarded her with this kind of acknowledgment. And as it turned out, her fourth Tony.

"They're on the mantle of our dear little house in county Cork," she reported when asked of the whereabouts of her three previous Tonys. "I'm bringing them back to put in my dressing room here."

For exactly one year Angela and *Sweeney Todd* hacked and splattered and belted their way into Broadway's heart. Yet strangely, the show that won eight Tonys never broke even financially.

"Marvelous as Sondheim's music and Harold Prince's staging were," Martin Gottfried wrote in *Broadway Musicals*, "*Sweeney Todd* was unsatisfying. It had no theatre purpose. The show's fate was all too familiar for this artistic team. It lost every cent even though it ran on Broadway for a year."

"There is, in fact, no serious social message in Sweeney," Richard Eder concluded. "At the end, when the cast lines up on the stage and points to us, singing that there are Sweeneys all about; the point is unproven."

Flawed though it might have been, *Sweeney Todd* answered to something audiences needed, and Richard Eder's final assessment of the show is just.

"There are defects, vital ones, but they are the failures of an extraordinary, fascinating, and often ravishingly lovely effort."

Angela also put her finger on it. "Life is very hard now for a great many people," she explained. "It's a natural tendency we've seen before—during hard times people seek escapist entertainment. The world needs to be entertained, to be taken out of itself, and musicals can do that."

And so, quite obviously, can she.

> *My fault as an actress is that I just go too far. I charac-*
> *terize myself right out of existence half the time . . .*
>
> *I wouldn't say the glamor thrills me—it fades terribly*
> *quickly. Growing up, growing older, you find your ideals*
> *and requirements change. Some people feel they have to ex-*
> *perience everything in life, and they're unhappy when they*
> *can't. I can get awfully excited about plain, ordinary*
> *things.*

*T*he seventies were winding down; a new decade was about to be-
gin, bringing with it a number of new directions. The following
March, Dorothy Loudon would be taking over Mrs. Lovett on
Broadway. Angela was to be in England for a few weeks shooting a
film. Then she and George Hearn were going on the road with
Sweeney Todd.

Meanwhile, there were the "plain, ordinary things" to occupy her
between shows—her increasing participation in a number of char-
itable organizations, especially AWAIC and drug abuse programs.
She was invited to Lenox Hill Hospital's Center for Communication
Disorders for a preview of their free screening program for speech,
voice and language disorders, a particular interest of hers since
Moyna's laryngectomy. The following year she headed a benefit for
AWAIC at the restaurant OnStage and taped a public service an-
nouncement for The Lighthouse, the New York Association for the
Blind, urging employers to hire visually handicapped workers.

Angela made no bones about her participation in these organizations. She saw a need, and offered to help, aware that her status as a

celebrity—and one who had survived a family crisis—attracted public attention to such causes.

"The area where I am most involved in social causes is child abuse and violence in the home," she explains. "I am on the board of the Family Rescue shelter for battered women and children in Chicago. Years ago those of us who were concerned about domestic violence could not get any attention. Now, thank God, the problems of child abuse and wife beating are out in the open."

There was also the occasional bit of just plain fun, like doing an ad for Blackglama mink, and the special honor of being nominated for *After Dark* magazine's 1979 Ruby Award. Named for Ruby Keeler, the Ruby Award was meant to be show business's accolade to one of its own as Performer of the Year. Usually *After Dark*'s editors culled nominees from a list of the year's bigger celebrities and voted among themselves. In 1979 the editors opened the voting to the public for the first time and the outcome surprised everybody. Winning out over such hot young stars as Richard Gere, Gilda Radner, Donna Summer, and even a write-in campaign for Barbra Streisand, was none other than Angela. The award was proof at last that she had audience recognition as well as staying power.

"My type is coming back," Angela explained pragmatically. "The Jane Fondas will be my age soon and they won't want to retire, so somebody will have to write roles for women of their age and experience to keep their careers going."

Her response was typically no-nonsense Angela. That didn't mean she wasn't deeply moved by the honor, or that she wouldn't wow them at the awards ceremony. She made quite an entrance at the Ruby Ball given in New York in December, 1979, looking "like a Sargent painting," as one reporter described her, in ruby-red velvet with puff sleeves and slinky skirt, designed by Bob Mackintosh, who had done costumes for both *Mame* and *Gypsy*.

As her soon-to-be-replacement in *Sweeney Todd*, Dorothy Loudon was selected to present Angela with the award. Angela was overcome by tears.

"We have two of the meanest girls in town here," Dorothy Loudon quipped, trying to lighten the moment.

Angela, recovering herself and taking her cue, responded, "I'm delighted Dorothy will be helping me out in the kitchen."

Confident she had left Mrs. Lovett in Dorothy Loudon's capable hands, Angela set about extricating herself temporarily from the role that had challenged her on so many different levels. Producers Mary Lea Johnson and Marty Richards held a big closing night party at Ted Hook's Backstage restaurant. Angela was off to England, with a last stopover at the Irish homestead.

"I knew I would never get back to leisurely life in Ireland when Hal Prince called to ask me to do *Sweeney Todd*," Angela said.

She and Peter sold the house the following year, bidding farewell to nearby neighbor Hurd Hatfield, Angela's costar in *Dorian Gray* who had introduced her and Peter all those years ago, and who had settled just down the road from them. It was time to say farewell to the river and the gently rolling countryside, to the heather and the rose gardens and the three-hundred-year-old elms.

Angela and Peter left Ireland with a good feeling, if not a little nostalgia. The Irish homestead had brought them together as a family during the hard times. By now the children were young adults, and both had turned out well. The strikingly attractive Deirdre, always the artistic one, had lived in New York for awhile and done some modeling. She had studied acting with the renowned Stella Adler and, at twenty-five, was married to photographer Rene Volpi. The couple were planning to move to Italy and open a restaurant.

Anthony, meanwhile, had directed a film during Angela's run in *The King And I,* and continued to pursue his acting career. He and his wife Lee were to make Angela a grandmother twice over. And David, the eldest, had settled in California and, after a brief stint as Angela's west coast agent, had carved himself a prosperous career as an architect and builder. Angela was proud of her children.

A farmhouse in upstate New York, a Manhattan apartment, and various temporary digs in Los Angeles and elsewhere, served as home for the next few years. The Shaws were gypsies once again. But by now Peter and Angela knew each other so well that home was wherever they happened to be—as long as Angela had her teapot and "a few potted plants."

When she left New York and *Sweeney Todd* behind in March of 1980, home became England, for the shooting of *The Mirror Crack'd*. This film could easily have been another forgettable movie for Angela. Certainly a number of all-too-familiar negative elements were present. There was the cast, top-heavy with big name stars, in which a lesser actress might easily have gotten lost. There was the makeup, which was to age her twenty years, a device that had worked against her since she was seventeen. There was a silly script device calling for her to sprain her ankle early on and so miss most of the action scenes.

The script itself was a weak rewrite of a remake of a tired genre best laid to rest with the demise of its master, Alfred Hitchcock. Angela also had to contend with the ghost of Margaret Rutherford, who in many people's minds was the only actress worthy of playing Agatha Christie's Miss Marple.

Angela found an elegant solution to this last problem.

"Miss Lansbury," movie critic Vincent Canby wrote in the *New York Times*, "asked to fill the sensible shoes of the late Margaret Rutherford, chooses not to compete with memory but to create what is virtually a different character. Hers is a sweet-natured, quick-witted but not especially eccentric Miss Marple."

How many times before had she taken a character someone else had created, found her own truth in it, and transformed it into an entirely different person? Her rationale was simple.

"The problem as an actress is to make Miss Marple's very plainness interesting. I never saw Dame Margaret, but I get the impression she played Miss Marple as a tweedy woman in gumboots always falling into duckponds. I play her absolutely straight. I'm trying to get at the woman Agatha Christie created: an Edwardian maiden lady imbued with great humanity and a mind of tremendous breadth. She's very exactly described in the books as tall, pale-complexioned, with twinkling blue eyes and white hair—not a fat galumph of a creature at all. I base my performance on that."

Not that it was easy. She had literally just stepped down from *Sweeney Todd*. It would have been easy to play Miss Marple as a caricature, particularly with Angela's dislike of restrained roles. Also, the genre lent itself to that kind of characterization, as had been demonstrated with varying degrees of success in *Mirror's* predecessors *Murder On The Orient Express* and *Death On The Nile*. But the old pro knew better.

"I played a cameo part of a drunken novelist in *Death On The Nile*, where I was able to come on and climb up the scenery," she explained, admitting to her ability to get carried away. "But I saw some of the early rushes here and realized I can't come bustling on as Miss Marple. I have to shut all the doors and shut off. And, after thirteen months of playing *Sweeney Todd*, I promise you that is not easy."

The job of an actress of Angela's calibre, of course, is to make it look easy. She did, to the point where the critics noticed how under-utilized she was in this film.

"It's an intelligent, legitimate performance," Vincent Canby acknowledged. "But nowhere near as entertaining as Miss Lansbury can be when she's playing to the top balcony."

"The worst sin of all," wrote Rex Reed, who was generally dissatisfied with *The Mirror Crack'd*, "is that this is a Marple story in which Marple has nothing much to do. If you're going to sprain her ankle in the first scene then send her home to knit doilies while everyone has all the fun—you don't need an actress of Lansbury's energy and resources. This grand but wasted actress could have phoned it in."

But she didn't. Holding her own in the stellar company of Elizabeth Taylor, Kim Novak, Rock Hudson, Tony Curtis, Geraldine Chaplin, and Edward Fox, she made Miss Marple believable. The movie's plot was the typical Agatha Christie mélange, a story-within-a-story about an American film crew shooting a movie in a sleepy English hamlet when a woman is murdered. It is Miss Marple's task, with the help of her detective nephew (Edward Fox) to unravel the clues.

Angela had no qualms about fixing the script just a little, adding character touches to Miss Marple to make her real. Instead of just knitting like some doddering old grandmother, Angela's Marple was a crossword fanatic, someone with a lucid mind who could think her way through a problem. And there was the controversy over the Turkish cigarettes.

"I felt that, as an Edwardian woman, she would do what my own grandmother did and always smoke a cigarette after dinner," Angela explained, all blue-eyed innocence. "It would be a Turkish cigarette, which she wouldn't inhale but simply use for a period of reflective calm."

Agatha Christie's daughter, visiting the set, was horrified at the idea and said as much. Angela lost that round, but not without a fight.

"I know they're all wrong, so I'm desperately searching for some other signal to let everyone know I'm thinking."

What might at first seem to be stubbornness, perhaps a bit of superstar theatrics, is significant on several levels. The film crew shot around Angela so that she only had to be on the set for two weeks. Anyone else would have caved in and, as Rex Reed suggested, "phoned in" her performance and gone home. But Angela was incapable of giving a half-hearted performance.

She could not have been aware of it, but a pattern was forming around these later years of her career, a pattern that was to bring her one of her biggest successes. It had begun with *Death On The Nile,* that overblown bit of pomposity in which she had done her very best to give a credible performance.

"Audiences found her to be the one bit of relief in that otherwise overheated desert drama," Stephen M. Silverman had written in the *New York Post,* and it was true. Audiences remembered Angela as the alcoholic murder mystery novelist, not just because she played it to the hilt, but because that was the way it was meant to be played. Now they were to be impressed with a totally different performance by the same actress in the same genre.

Take a murder mystery novelist and eliminate the alcoholism. Make her also an amateur sleuth, like Miss Marple, with an uncanny knack for stumbling onto the scene of the crime. Find an actress who has played both roles on the large screen, and who also has the ability to take a live audience and hold it in the palm of her hand, and dare to bring her to the small screen. The result—a little thing called "Murder, She Wrote."

But "Murder, She Wrote" was still several years in the future as Angela finished her stint in *The Mirror Crack'd* and began to warm up for another go at *Sweeney Todd*. She immersed herself in the work at hand and, as always, managed to find a little fun. One such moment was her reunion with Elizabeth Taylor. It had been thirty-six years since *National Velvet*.

"She was eleven and I was eighteen and I was very conscious of the age gap," Angela admits. "Don't forget I'd already played the maid in *Gaslight* and been out on the road doing cabaret, and here I was playing a fifteen-year-old, which I felt was slightly demeaning.

"But," she remembers, "I did see Elizabeth on the M-G-M lot after that, and I always took an affectionate interest in her."

As for their reunion, thirty-six years later and with Angela aged almost a quarter of a century on top of that, she said, "Well, I was sitting in the lunch tent in costume when I suddenly looked across and there was Elizabeth with a couple of other people. I said 'Elizabeth, how good to see you.' She looked at me totally blankly and I said 'It's Angela.' She yelled out 'Angela—I wouldn't have recognized you in a million years.' Which says something about my makeup."

Also a member of the reunion was Kim Novak, with whom Angela had worked in *Moll Flanders*. Angela joked, "She did Elizabeth and me dirty by losing twenty pounds."

But once again, no matter how many superstars were crammed into a movie around her, it was Angela the critics noticed.

"In her belted blue cardigan, ankle-length skirt, sensible lace-up shoes and gray felt hat, she looked like everyone's maiden aunt," Michael Billington wrote in the *Times*. "But as she and Rock Hudson went off to examine a corpse, there was something in the way her head craned eagerly forward and in the thrusting, expectant incline of her trunk that conjured up those indomitable English spinsters encountered on a windswept Acropolis, hungrily sniffing out information about fifth-century Athens."

It was the same characteristic Clive Barnes had called her use of "emblematic gesture" and "sense of heightened naturalism" when he encountered it on the stage. If Angela's talent can be reduced to its essence, it is this ability to find the tiniest truth in a character, in something as seemingly insignificant as a gesture, a craning of the neck, a posture, and use it to make the audience see the whole character.

Acting teachers joke about the "less is more" school of acting. But Angela's training comes from life.

"Actors and actresses are rather like sponges," is how she puts it. "The more you soak up, the more you are enhanced as a performer."

> *I'd hate to be starting out today. It's difficult for young actors and actresses now. There's a style of acting—I call it shorthand acting—that's effective, but mostly visual, enhanced and created in most instances by camera work. The young performers are all wonderful-looking, but not too much is being asked of them in the way of acting. It doesn't matter what role they're playing; there's a sameness in the style. I worry desperately for them.*

*B*ack in harness, Angela and George Hearn took *Sweeney Todd* on the road. From Washington, D.C., to Philadelphia, Boston, Chicago, San Francisco, and finally Los Angeles, Sweeney and his bloody inamorata carved their way across the country for eleven months. The tour was both lucrative and comfortable.

"*Sweeney Todd* has opened a lot of new doors for me," Angela confided. "I'll make much more on the road than I did on Broadway."

She earned every cent of it. Angela was still good box office. When the show opened at the Dorothy Chandler Pavilion in Los Angeles, good reviews and word of mouth brought in two million dollars in advance sales. And the audiences on the road got as good a show as Broadway audiences.

One would have thought an exhausted Angela would sit home and rest on her laurels indefinitely, but within a few months of *Sweeney's* close she was off to England to do the movie version of Joseph Papp's brilliant staging of Gilbert and Sullivan's *The Pirates Of Penzance.*

For some reason no one had ever attempted to film *Pirates* before. The show Joe Papp characterized as a "classy classic" had survived in repertory for one hundred and three years, performed by everyone from international Gilbert and Sullivan societies to community theater groups. Such extremes of performance had earned it a mixed reputation, but under Papp's aegis it had enjoyed a rollickingly successful Broadway run. There was no reason not to try it on film. Papp kept his cast of exuberant young pirates and pretties—and the irrepressible, ever-young George Rose—intact in the transition from Broadway to the screen, with one exception. The exception was Angela.

The premise of *Pirates* revolves around a misunderstanding. Young Frederic (Rex Smith) is apprenticed to a pirate band, apparently because of his father's deathbed wish. The elderly gentleman confided this wish to Frederic's faithful but hard-of-hearing nursemaid, Ruth. Mistaking her master's instructions to apprentice young Frederic to a *pilot,* Ruth has him apprenticed to a *pirate,* and the King of the Pirates at that.

As the doting nanny Ruth, Angela refused to get lost in all the swashbuckling. Kevin Kline as the Pirate King, the lovely Linda Ronstadt as the love of Frederic's life, and George Rose as Major-General Stanley, the "Modern Major General" were highly visible against a supporting cast of over forty singers. But Angela held her own. Her Ruth, cooking and cleaning for this band of rogues, making wishful cow-eyes at the grown-up Frederic (who is a well-turned out lad, thanks to her), falls somewhere between the prim Miss Price of *Bedknobs And Broomsticks,* and the lusty, waggish Mrs. Lovett. And, oh, can she sing!

"In *Pirates* I was singing out of my range and just got away with it by the skin of my teeth," Angela claims. "Mine is not really a trained voice, you know."

She could have fooled the critics. William Schwenk Gilbert's lyrics consist mostly of stanza upon stanza of staccato tongue twisters. Most people can't speak them, much less sing them. Against Sir Arthur Sullivan's almost operatic music, they present quite a challenge. Angela was up to the challenge. She had cut her musical teeth on Sondheim, after all. Gilbert and Sullivan was cake and ale.

In *Newsday*, Alex Keneas wrote, "Angela Lansbury's Ruth, biting every word, is a special delight, since some of the phrasing is less than pristine."

And Archer Winston of the *New York Post*, blissfully bypassing the young folk, singled out George Rose and Angela as singing "with distinction in the tradition of Gilbert and Sullivan, that is, fast, stylized and expressive."

The Pirates of Penzance can be credited with offering Angela a number of related opportunities. Suddenly her vocal abilities were very much in demand. She was asked to do the voice of Mommy Fortuna in Lord Lew Grade's animated film *The Last Unicorn.* She shared voice-over credit with Alan Arkin, Tammy Grimes, Christopher Lee, Mia Farrow, and others in one of the better children's films to be released in recent years. And the prestigious London Records invited her to be part of the cast recording a new version of *The Beggar's Opera.*

This last offer rather terrified her. Not only was this to be a new performing version of the John Gay classic, reworked by the distinguished conductor Richard Bonynge and Douglas Gamley, but the cast read like a show business and operatic *Who's Who* including Graham Clarke, Michael Hordern, Kiri Te Kanawa, James Morris, Regina Resnik, Anthony Rolf-Johnson, and Joan Sutherland. It was enough to make anyone breathless.

For once the old pro had doubts. She would have to sing in a studio with this distinguished cast, unseen, unable to project any of her visual acting ability into the character of Mrs. Peachum. She would have to hold her own solely with her voice. Could she do it?

"The producers wanted a voice with a lot of character for Mrs. Peachum, and I was immensely pleased to be asked to do it," Angela says. "Next to acting I love music best, but I felt I had no business on the same platform with the opera singers Kiri Te Kanawa, James Morris, and Joan Sutherland, who were in the cast."

But she was game, and just to prove that there's no people like show people, the others in the cast gave her their complete support. They seemed to feel that she, as the musical actress, had the advantage.

"They made me feel that it gave me an edge, bless their hearts," Angela remembers warmly. "They were in fear and trembling for the acting, just as I was in fear and trembling for the vocal side of it."

The mutual admiration society bolstered each other's courage, and the recording session worked like a charm. She added, "It turned out well, and the English critics liked it."

This recording of *The Beggar's Opera* was enough of a success to earn Angela an offer from Original Cast Records to record a less successful show, the late and not overly lamented *Prettybelle*. Like the original cast recording of *Anyone Can Whistle,* this was an interesting addition to Angela's growing number of recordings, as well as an important contribution to the history of musical theater. Regardless of the relative merits of any Broadway-bound show, it deserves to be recorded for posterity. In decades to come, when no other record remains of the Broadway musical than perhaps a few production photographs, these recordings will prove invaluable.

These recordings were also a success in that they made Angela determined someday to record her very first song, "Goodbye, Little Yellow Bird" from *The Picture of Dorian Gray.*

"It was the first time the public heard that thin, pure little voice," she says, able to detach herself from the tremulous, vulnerable eighteen-year-old who sang the song so many years ago. "It pleases me enormously that people remember the song. Some have even taped it when the picture was shown on TV."

Angela has yet to make that particular recording, though she was soon to immortalize the song in quite a different context.

A Little Family Business, Angela's first crack at a straight play on Broadway since *A Taste Of Honey* over twenty years before, again proved that there's no such thing as a sure thing, particularly where Broadway is concerned.

All the right elements seemed present—a light, topical comedy written by a highly successful screenwriter, not one but two veteran directors, and a brand new character for Angela to discover and bring to life in her unique way. But one thing anyone in theater knows is that the whole is not always equal to the sum of its creative parts.

Based on a French boulevard comedy that had been running successfully in Paris for two years, *A Little Family Business* tried to aim right at the heart, and the pocketbook, of the American hoi polloi. With Broadway ticket prices beginning to climb to astronomical heights, producers wanted something that would grab the middle class and make them not only buy tickets, but tell their neighbors to do the same.

The play was to appeal to the American small businessman worried about foreign competition, specifically, the Japanese. This premise was much to the show's detriment. The plot was very simple; a New England businessman, the self-made owner of a small carpet-sweeper factory and full time bigot, suffers a heart attack and can no longer work. His dotty, sheltered wife, who has never worked outside the home, must hold off the tide of "those pushy buck-toothed little stinkers" and save the family business.

The biggest no-no should have been obvious from the beginning. What comes out of Archie Bunker's mouth, aimed at a television audience, can be laughed at in the privacy of one's own home. Shot from the lip of even a veteran actor like John McMartin, given silent assent by his prim stage wife, and aimed for the last row of the balcony, the same jingoistic diatribe is going to raise eyebrows, not applause. Theater audiences won't admit to enjoying such crude humor, at least not in public.

The play was to open in Los Angeles at the Ahmanson Theater for a six-week run, then head for Broadway just before Christmas. There were production problems from the first.

Playwright Jay Presson Allen, whose screenplays included *Funny Lady, Cabaret, Prince Of The City* and the books for *Cactus Flower* and *Forty Carats,* ran into some artistic differences in her first venture with a stage play. Artistic difference number one was director Vivian Matalon. Matalon, whose previous credits included *A Song At Twilight, After The Rain, The Square Root Of Wonderful* and *Mornings At Seven,* was no amateur. Whatever the actual difficulties were remains unclear—possibly Matalon, anticipating trouble, suggested softening some of the dialogue—but three weeks into rehearsals, Jay Presson Allen was quoted as saying there were some "very, very big production problems."

Angela would only say diplomatically: "We don't have it all yet."

The upshot was that Vivian Matalon was replaced three days before the Los Angeles opening by playwright/lyricist Martin Charnin, whose last major credit had been as director/lyricist for the musical *Annie.*

Charnin was directing a revue in New York at the time and was unable to leave. He somehow managed to direct *Family Business* long distance from the east coast, intending to put some finishing touches on it when it got to New York.

Following a hellish rehearsal schedule, last minute rewrites, direction in absentia, and a protest by the Japanese-American League, *A Little Family Business* opened at the Ahmanson on October 8, 1982 to vicious reviews. Possibly it was the furor stirred up by the Japanese-American League that resulted in every daily (except the *San Fernando Valley Daily News*) rushing like lemmings to pan the show. The League protested what it considered inherent racism in the script and suggested that at least one sympathetic Japanese character be written in. The producers balked at their suggestions, and eliminated only one particularly racist line from the script. The bad feeling lingered.

In truth, *A Little Family Business* didn't just single out the Japanese. In a failed attempt at Archie Bunker reverse-psychology it hurled insults at Italians, homosexuals and anyone else within range. The attempt was to shock the audience, make them laugh, and make them think. The attempt failed. The critics were shocked. The audiences laughed, but they didn't think.

"As at a party when someone commits a really unforgivable gaffe," Dan Sullivan wrote in the *Los Angeles Times*, "The inclination is to steal away from Angela Lansbury and *A Little Family Business*, resolved not to say a word about it."

The show was also lambasted by the *Herald Examiner*. Angela was flabbergasted. "I'm absolutely floored by them," she said. "I didn't expect any critic to love it, but they didn't sit there and listen and watch. The audiences are loving it."

Obviously she was putting a brave face on it. At the same time she wondered if she wasn't the problem, rather than the play. It was a rerun of *Dear World* all over again. "I'm worried that I may be the fly in the ointment," she confided to reporters, "because I'm usually associated with more artistic kinds of affairs."

Objectively, of course, she could hardly be blamed for the show's weaknesses. If anything, she should have gotten some kind of award for sheer determination. A lesser trouper would have pulled out early when personality clashes turned the production into a shambles, but Angela hung on. Doubtless she believed in the shock value of the dialogue, or she would not have consented to do such a controversial play.

She had personal as well as professional reasons for sticking to her guns. Not only was this the first nonmusical role she'd been offered in a long time that really called upon her talents, but she had a family member in the cast.

Theater-goers might have noted the name "Anthony Shaw" in the program next to the role of Scott. But unless they knew Angela's family life fairly well, they would not have realized he was her son. The fact that Scott was also Angela's son in the play was serendipitous. "One of those lovely occasions in life that happens every now and then," as Angela put it.

She had had absolutely no influence in getting Anthony the role, and in fact knew nothing about it until after he'd auditioned and gotten the part. "Anthony was chosen before I knew he was being considered for the role," she declared, revealing that they had both promised during rehearsals not to get in each other's way nor criticize each other's performance. "But," she hinted mischievously, "I expect we'll each get hell from the other if we blow our lines."

Angela was insistent that playbills in Los Angeles and in New York make no mention whatsoever of the relationship between her and Anthony. "Absolutely on purpose," she declared. "It's hard sometimes to surface when you're drowned in the reputation of your mother."

She was particularly concerned about Anthony for another reason. He and his wife Lee were expecting their first baby in early December, around the time that *Family Business* would be previewing in New York. When Lee gave birth to Peter John Shaw at 5:20 A.M. on the morning of December 8, Anthony had been with her at Lenox Hill Hospital all night, rushing there immediately after the performance.

"He hasn't been to sleep," grandmother Angela reported. "He hasn't even eaten, but he's going on tonight!"

Asked how she felt about her new role as a grandmother, Angela was exuberant. "I feel like a million dollars, just fabulous. This is my first grandchild and one of the most exciting things that's ever happened to me. I can't wait to see him." She did manage to do just that between the matinee and the evening performance.

Trailing its bad reviews behind it, *A Little Family Business* opened in New York at the Martin Beck Theater. Producers could only hope the critics wouldn't pan it here as well. Holding court in her dressing room (the same one Elizabeth Taylor had recently vacated following *Little Foxes*; it still bore Liz's trademark decor—violet shutters and ceiling-high mirrors), Angela waited for the reviews.

While she waited, she received a surprise visit from Bette Davis, with whom she had recently costarred in a television miniseries, "Little Gloria, Happy At Last," about the childhood of Gloria Vanderbilt. Miss Davis was extremely gracious about the night's performance. "You could have played all the parts I played," she declared magnanimously.

Once again, New York critics knew how to separate a good performance from a flawed play. The *Daily News* reported that Angela had received a standing ovation on opening night, and stated that her "scintillating role as today's grandma had women cheering and laughing."

In the *Post,* under the headline BUSINESS SUCCEEDS BY REALLY TRYING, Clive Barnes called *Family Business* an "excessively flimsy boulevard comedy," but praised Angela's Lillian as "sweetly smiling as a benevolent New England matriarch whose interests range from Nieman-Marcus catalogues to whale saving."

It was Frank Rich's critique in the *New York Times* that was the most bitter. "It would be unjust to say that *A Little Family Business,* the comedy that brought Angela Lansbury back to Broadway last night, is the worst production in a poor theater season," he wrote. "Let's just say that *A Little Family Business* is the season's worst nonmusical play. It's definitely the thing to see once you've exhausted all the all-night movies on 42nd Street."

Rich lambasted everything from the script to the supporting cast to the direction, which he credited to Martin Charnin, despite the fact that Charnin, while his name appeared in the program, steadfastly refused to take any responsibility for his three days of transcontinental direction either in Los Angeles or in New York. "Martin Charnin's direction is so coarse that, next to this play, a typical episode of 'I Love Lucy' looks as if it had been produced by the Comedie Francaise," Rich declared.

He found fault with star John McMartin, accusing him of mugging his way through the role, and hated Angela's character of Lillian, whom he described as "dithering." However, try as he might, he couldn't find fault with Angela. "Miss Lansbury admirably keeps her wits about her and looks fetching in a wide variety of Theoni V. Aldredge gowns," Rich said.

He was trying to be cool, even cruel, but he couldn't. Broadway critics have traditionally adored Angela, and with good reason. Frank Rich finally surrendered and told his readers why. "In the best of the four or five good moments she's allowed, she does a delicate piece of mime in which, with the crossing of her legs and repositioning of her head, she instantly transforms herself from a sedentary hausfrau into a proper business executive," he reports, capturing the essence of that less-is-more gift that is Angela's trademark.

"But," Rich concludes almost sympathetically, "only a sadist could enjoy watching this angelic actress dance on the head of so nasty a little pin."

> *If I'm going to do television, I'm going to bring all my experience and specialization to it, plus the expertise one hopes to pick up along the way.*

A *Little Family Business* had on the whole been an unpleasant experience. It seemed to suggest that it was time to give Broadway a rest. There didn't seem to be any enticing movie roles on the horizon at the moment either. Angela took a second look at a medium she hadn't seriously considered in almost twenty years.

"Quite frankly, I was never offered a leading television role commensurate with my experience. Over the years I was offered series, but the role would always be as a member of some ensemble group in a situation comedy. As I told my agent, I didn't work forty years to come along and support someone I don't even know. If that's what TV was going to mean, I'd have to forget it."

While a guest spot on a television series had no appeal, several meaningful roles in TV miniseries captured Angela's attention in the early eighties. The first of these was the NBC-TV two-parter "Little Gloria, Happy At Last," based on the Barbara Goldsmith bestseller about the old-money Vanderbilts and their marital and family entanglements.

The plot centered around the custody battle over ten-year-old Gloria Vanderbilt when her parents' marriage broke up and both sets of grandparents took each other to court in order to have her live with them. The cast was impressive, including Bette Davis as Alice Vanderbilt, Gloria's paternal grandmother, and Glynis Johns as Laura Morgan, the maternal grandmother. Gray eminence Barnard

155

Hughes was to play the judge who decides to award custody of little Gloria to her aunt, Gertrude Vanderbilt Whitney.

Angela played Gertrude Vanderbilt Whitney as a warm, genteel, loving aunt, more concerned with her small niece's needs than with the power struggles within the family. Her portrayal won her an Emmy nomination, her first. The miniseries was shot against the backdrop of the old Whitney and Vanderbilt mansions in Newport, Rhode Island.

Angela's next television venture took her to Europe for the shooting of "Lace," ABC's five-hour miniseries based on a recent bestseller, about the coming-of-age adventures of three boarding-school girls. Angela played a character outside her usual range, the flamboyant French aunt of one of the girls, and enjoyed the chance to try on an accent. "Lace" was shot in several exotic locales, including Paris, the French Alps, and Lausanne.

Her third TV venture was in a tiny role in "The Olympic Games: Athens, 1896," in which she played the mother of Olympic medalist Alice Garrett.

Meanwhile, *Sweeney Todd* had been filmed for the Public Broadcasting System and was showing on cable TV stations. It won four awards for cablecasting excellence, and Angela received her second Emmy nomination for Mrs. Lovett.

Getting her feet wet in several miniseries had proved rewarding, and Angela subsequently signed to do two television movies in 1983. One was "The Gift Of Love: A Christmas Story," which was to reunite her with her extremely gifted costar from *The Long Hot Summer* and *Anyone Can Whistle,* Lee Remick.

"The Gift Of Love" managed to avoid some of the sticky sentiment characteristic of Christmas specials. In it a family faces bankruptcy and the closing of the small department store they have owned for several generations. The store's last few days of business, the letting go of so many faithful employees—one in a Santa Claus suit—as well as the crisis within the family itself, are milked for all they're worth. But a strong performance on Miss Remick's part and the warmth and wisdom of the family matriarch save "The Gift Of Love" from being pure mush.

Of Angela's portrayal of the matriarch, the *Daily News*'s Kay Gardella said, "Her wise and devoted mother, Amanda Fenwick, is played deliciously." Gardella went so far as to credit Angela with being the movie's saving grace. "Lansbury is a strong force; she has the ability to pull a script up by its bootstraps and send it on its way. She puts life, vigor and meaning into a role, and her lilting voice is a delight to hear."

Her second television movie, "A Talent For Murder," gave Angela a chance to work with Sir Laurence Olivier. Originally it had been a stage play on Broadway in 1981, starring Claudette Colbert. The televised version was being produced for the Showtime cable network. In it Anne Royce McClain, the world's most famous mystery writer, wheelchair-ridden and a bit of an alcoholic, has to prevent her greedy family from either murdering her or having her declared senile and put in a home.

It was a baroque, hammy role, but Angela gave it a go. The production was shot on a very tight schedule, and the result was a stiff, rickety movie that looked too much like the stage version. Nevertheless, TV critics like Kay Gardella found it "totally amusing."

And then there was Olivier. He played Mrs. McClain's husband with a dry, wry humor that proved he could be just as much the ham as anyone else. Angela adored him.

"There's nobody who's more giving," she declares. "He's a very grand gentleman of the theater. Even so, it wasn't easy to make the play work." But for a chance to work with a living legend, it was worth it.

*I*n a Broadway gone moribund somewhere in the late seventies, revival was the name of the game. Only tourists and expense-account types could afford the price of a ticket anymore, and these were hardly the audience to sit still for anything new and different. Composer/lyricist Jerry Herman, always a crowd-pleaser, had had a recent success with the revival of *Little Me*. Why not try *Mame* one more time?

There was no question as to who would play the title role. Producer Mitch Leigh "wanted Angela, period."

Angela, finished with "A Talent For Murder" and perhaps wondering if that was all there was to television, could hardly refuse. *Mame* had always been her good-luck talisman. The limited tour in 1972 had gotten her back on her creative feet after she'd picked up the pieces of her personal life and painstakingly put them back together. It had given her the courage to come on like gangbusters in *Gypsy*, blowing away any notion that she might be out to pasture permanently. Maybe *Mame* could do as much for her again. Even if it didn't, playing everybody's favorite aunt could still be a damned good time.

With Angela signed, it was surprisingly easy to round up almost all of the "old gang" who had made the magic in 1966. Jane Connell was to play Agnes Gooch once more. Sab Shimono would recreate Ito the sagacious houseboy, and Willard Waterman and John C. Becher would reprise their wonderful villains. Anne Francine, one of the first to take over the role of Vera Charles from Bea Arthur, would have Vera all to herself this time.

The challenge was to preserve as much of the flavor of the original as possible without turning the show into a museum piece. Director John Bowab tried to stay as true to Gene Saks' original direction as possible. Choreographer Diana Baffa-Baill, who had been a chorus dancer in the original production, managed to recapture much of Onna White's 1966 choreography. Even Peter Wolf's scenery was based on the William and Jean Eckhardt sketches for the original. Robert Mackintosh gave new life to his original costume designs, with the help of a costume budget that included $400,000 just for furs by Maximilian.

As for Angela, she remembered every line of every song as if it had been yesterday.

"The only difference," she told a reporter for the *New York Post,* "is my figure. It now bunches up in the middle, and that's hard to get rid of. I'm dieting. Half portions of everything. I'm losing only half a pound a week, but I'm losing."

Mame went into rehearsals in June, 1983. The plan was to open in San Diego, with out-of-town tryouts in Philadelphia and Boston before opening at the former Uris—now renamed Gershwin—Theater in New York. Weak ticket sales in Philadelphia hastened the New York opening. On July 24, 1983, *Mame* and Angela were the toast of Broadway once again.

Clive Barnes had this reaction: "The present revival—which sent Saturday night's preview audience almost dotty with joy—is a seemingly punctilious restaging of the 1966 original. Not unexpectedly some spontaneity has been lost, to be replaced by a certain degree of reverence."

Frank Rich was a little less kind. "The new production at the Gershwin Theater looks like an almost exact replica of the musical that opened at the Winter Garden in 1966," he wrote in the *Times*. "But though the pieces of *Mame* have been retrieved from the past, one doesn't find the present-tense heat that might again weld them into a fresh, effortless entertainment."

Both critics were in agreement, however, on their amazement at the ageless, effortless Angela. "Assisted by the still-undimmed effulgence of Miss Angela Lansbury," Barnes wrote, "*Mame* is back in town. The sheer radiance of Miss Lansbury remains intact—sensationally intact."

And Frank Rich pinpointed what had had the preview audience cheering. "Angela Lansbury is back as Patrick Dennis's high-living, free-thinking aunt—still kicking a leg clear to heaven in the irresistible title song, still pouring her soul into the ballad 'If He Walked into My Life,' still exhorting one and all to 'Live, live, live!' When Miss Lansbury locks arms with Mr. Shimono and Miss Connell to strut to 'We Need a Little Christmas,' you could swear that time has stood still."

Angela still had the old magic. She must have taken a little piece of it home with her every night, because it was about to bring her into the hearts and homes of a bigger audience than she had ever reached before.

> *It was the first role I could imagine myself doing. Everything was right there. I could have devised the character of Jessica Beatrice Fletcher myself. I have a feeling she's the kind of a person that most people who are familiar with my work will like.*

"Murder, She Wrote" caught Angela completely by surprise. Television had been the furthest thing from her mind.

"The theater has always had first call on my talents. I genuinely thrill to the excitement of a live audience, and I have had very little desire to do television or films in recent years."

The revival of *Mame* had closed after a disappointingly short run, and there was rumored to be a musical version of *Sunset Boulevard* in the works just for Angela. When it didn't materialize, she was temporarily left stranded with no new prospects on the immediate horizon.

"Within the week, I was sent two television scripts," reports the star who had steadfastly balked at television series all those years. "One was a situation comedy from Norman Lear and the other was the two-hour pilot for 'Murder, She Wrote.'"

There was no question as to which one she would turn down right away. But the other wasn't as easy to refuse. Angela's instincts told her to take her time over this one, even though she was not the first actress to be offered the role. Writer/producer Peter Fischer had originally written it for Jean Stapleton.

That made good television sense. Miss Stapleton, a veteran television performer, was familiar to millions of viewers as Edith Bunker from "All In The Family."

161

"But she had just lost her husband and didn't want to do any-thing," Angela explains. "When I read it, I felt that Peter's script could have been written for me. Besides, there are so few decent roles for women on television, and I was immediately taken by Jessica."

At first glance, Jessica Beatrice Fletcher may seem to be half "American Miss Marple," as Angela described her in an early inter-view, and half fictional version of the real-life creator of Miss Mar-ple, Dame Agatha Christie. But the resemblance is superficial.

Miss Marple was a terribly English spinster. Jessica Fletcher is all-American, a widow and substitute teacher living in a backwater town on the coast of Maine. When her nephew finds the manuscript of a murder mystery she's been scribbling in her spare time and sends it to a New York publisher, the result is overnight success. "J.B. Fletcher" becomes a best-selling novelist who travels all over the country doing book tours and enjoying her newfound wealth and celebrity. An amateur sleuth, she always seems to stumble onto the scene of a just-committed murder and invariably solves the crime.

The two-hour pilot for "Murder, She Wrote" was called "The Death of Sherlock Holmes," and it set the pattern for the entire series. In it, Jessica is invited to the home of her publisher (Arthur Hill) to attend a costume party. When a party guest dressed as Sher-lock Holmes is found floating face down in the swimming pool, Jessica's nephew Grady becomes the prime suspect and she goes into action to establish his innocence.

The formula was a common one in the early days of television dramatic series, popularized by "Perry Mason" over a quarter of a century before. But present day television audiences are more used to passive entertainment and don't necessarily want to be challenged by plots that keep them as much in the dark as the characters, that tease them with clues and red herrings and dare them to work out the mystery themselves. The last show to try the whodunit formula had been "The Adventures Of Ellery Queen," and it had met with only modest success. The producers of "Murder, She Wrote" were taking a big risk.

They had as their consultants Richard Levinson and William

Link, cocreators of "Columbo," the murder mystery series starring Peter Falk that had worked for years, but the whodunit formula wasn't the only risk they were taking.

Dramatic series starring women as principal characters are traditionally doomed to failure. Even when the star is young and sexy, as Anne Francis in "Honey West," Lynda Carter in "Wonder Woman," Lindsay Wagner in "The Bionic Woman" or Angie Dickinson in "Policewoman," viewer acceptance is mixed. In the case of Jessica Fletcher, producers were going against type by creating a middle-aged principal character and casting an actress who was not a well-known television star.

"We were getting condolences before we even went on the air," according to creator Richard Levinson. "At best, we hoped that it would be a marginal success."

CBS-TV's programming department did one very clever thing. They put "Murder, She Wrote" in the Sunday-night time slot directly following "60 Minutes," a show that attracted a mature, intelligent audience. If these people could be persuaded not to turn their televisions off as soon as "60 Minutes" was over, "Murder, She Wrote" might find itself with a built-in viewership.

The gamble paid off. For one thing, the rival networks had programs like "Knight Rider" and "Hardcastle and McCormick" in the same time slot. These shows were aimed at an entirely different audience. More important, "Murder, She Wrote" was high quality entertainment.

"Not taking itself very seriously," *New York Times* columnist John J. O'Connor wrote, "'Murder, She Wrote' is a pleasant, almost old-fashioned entertainment, and it does not require a single screeching car chase. Miss Lansbury keeps the character on a remarkably attractive course. At one point she even manages to get in a few moments of touching romance."

The *Times* critic touched on several of the strong points that had drawn Angela to the role in the first place. "I abhor violence," she told an interviewer early in the series. "We're not tilting in that direction. You'll hear about the murders, but won't see them. If there's any soapbox that I would climb on, it would be to cut down on the amount of violence on television. Our program is a detective yarn. It's not about violence; it's about the pitting of the minds."

There was that, but there was also the character of Jessica Fletcher herself. "There's nothing like a good villainess," says the actress who should know. "You can go to town and chew on great chunks of scenery. But some of the most successful things that I've done have been playing the simplest possible women. My sense is that Jessica Fletcher is very open, resilient and brave, a woman of very strong moral character. But she's not a bore. Jessica is an innately sophisticated person, even though she's from a small village in Maine. She's very well educated and fits in everywhere. I represent a huge chunk of the viewing audience: the middle-aged woman," Angela concludes. "She's not very often represented as a vital and intelligent being."

As of the beginning of the 1984 television season, all that was to change. The biggest obstacle had been convincing the star herself. Angela admits to her residual snobbery about television.

"I had been propositioned by a television executive five or six years before," she says. "Taken to dinner at '21' and told if I ever wanted to . . . I looked at him askance. I was in *Sweeney Todd*. I couldn't imagine I would ever want to do television."

"Murder's" producers were equally skeptical about Angela at first. When Jean Stapleton turned down the role of Jessica Fletcher and someone mentioned Angela Lansbury as a possibility, the reaction was "She's not about to do television. She's a Broadway actress."

But what she calls the "slew of roles in miniseries," starting with "Little Gloria," changed Angela's mind. "I began to sense that the television audience was very receptive to me, and I decided I should stop flirting and shut the door or say to my agents, 'I'm ready to think Series.'"

Her readiness and the right series happily coincided. "Murder, She Wrote" was launched in September, 1984, and the results amazed everybody. Not only did it hold on, it outlasted the ratings wars and was picked up for a second season. And then it really took off.

It opened the 1985 season occupying the same time slot as Stephen Spielberg's "Amazing Stories," which was premiering on NBC. Experts waited for the brainchild of the director of *Star Wars, Close Encounters* . . . , etc., to blow staid little "Murder, She Wrote" right out of the water. The first week, "Amazing Stories" ranked twelfth in the Nielsen ratings; "Murder, She Wrote" held its own at sixth. By the following Sunday, "Amazing Stories" had slumped to twenty-fourth, and "Murder, She Wrote" climbed to fourth in the ratings.

"Based on the current opposition, 'Murder, She Wrote' will dominate its time period this year," Senior Vice President of Programming Harvey Shephard was quoted as saying.

"I was sure some of our audience would go to Spielberg out of curiosity," Executive Producer Peter Fischer says. "But, instead, two and a half million more people are watching us each week this year."

Network executives attribute the unlooked-for success to several factors. "It's a matter of youth versus maturity," Fischer says. "And generally, maturity seems to be winning out. There's been a big change in TV viewing habits lately. The kid stuff is losing favor because the teens and subteens are watching MTV or youth-oriented movies on tape, and many of them have dropped out of the Nielsen network-viewing audience."

Besides, adds Fischer, "Angela is a class act."

Angela's long-time friend, *Gypsy* coproducer Fritz Holt, concurs. "Any project where Angela is involved, everyone seems to class up. She's very demanding, but of herself first. I know that with 'Murder' she takes home next week's lines to decide if her character would say what's in the script. She brings her great taste to any project; that's why her show is so good."

Angela's perfectionism starts with herself and the character of Jessica Fletcher, but it extends to every aspect of the show as well.

"When it comes to 'Murder, She Wrote,' I'm a combination hawk and mother hen, and it's my baby," Angela insists. In between checking on the sets, the lighting, and the sound, she makes certain there's nothing in the script that Jessica wouldn't do.

One script called for her to do a scene in a nightgown and robe while the sheriff, played by Martin Milner, sits in front of her fire-place in a blanket waiting for his clothes to dry. Angela decided Jessica wouldn't be dressed like that with a man in the room, and called producer Robert F. O'Neill at home at nine o'clock at night to tell him as much. The script was changed. Another time she wrangled with director Philip Leacock over a line in which Jessica has to ask a doctor about a particular poison. Angela maintained that, as a mystery writer, Jessica would know about such things. The line was changed.

As far as her fellow performers are concerned, Angela can some-times seem like a bully. It's just that she can't abide amateurism. She doesn't see why television performers can't measure up to the stringent artistic demands that theater actors make of themselves. "Too many young performers take their responsibilities and duties with a very casual attitude," Angela states.

Of her weekly guest stars she said, "When you deal with so many egos every week, you have to make sure the guests understand that cooperation is a must. It would become chaotic quite quickly if I didn't take charge. I've shouted a few times, and I've told people to shape up, because we've got to keep characters' credibility high. I know that some directors might want to strangle me from time to time. But there are times when I know they appreciate my taking charge, because there's just no time to tolerate anyone trying to play Star of the Week."

If anyone is entitled to this attitude, it's Angela, because it's due to her sheer professionalism. As another friend observes, "There's no ego with Angela. She put in her time *not* being a star."

> *I have no social life and am rarely alone with my husband. Heavens, I'm a nun for television! Why am I doing this to myself?*
>
> *In "Murder, She Wrote" I often think of myself as Bugs Bunny: I have to run in and grab the evidence, race out in a cloud of dust and return to say: "That's all, folks!"*

She gets up between 5:15 and 5:30 A.M. and heads for the studio by 6:15. The day's shooting starts at 8:00. She has fallen asleep over her script the night before, and brushes up her lines in the car. Reading in a moving vehicle used to make her carsick; now it's one of the few peaceful moments in her day. These days she swears she has to make an appointment to trim her own toenails.

She selects her own wardrobe for the show, does all her own makeup, and cuts and dyes her own hair, although she will accept touch-ups from a studio hairdresser just before she goes on.

"It's my training from the theater," she says. "You must learn to take care of yourself or you become a slave to other people's time. Not that everyone does their own hair and makeup, mind you," she adds mischievously. "Elizabeth Taylor certainly doesn't. But then, she's good at other things."

In her dressing room on the lot, a frostily air conditioned trailer with comfortable chairs and coordinated curtains, wearing her "lucky" dressing gown, embroidered with good wishes from the cast of *Gypsy,* she is assisted by Dolores Childers, who has been her dresser since *Mame* in 1966. Hovering in the background is the rest of her support group: son Anthony, who is dialogue coach for the show, and Peter.

The job of the dialogue coach on "Murder, She Wrote" is to see to it that the natives of Cabot Cove, Maine retain their New England accents. With regulars like Tom Bosley and William Windom, who have lived in town all their lives, the accents are necessarily thicker. Jessica Fletcher, who has traveled a great deal, has a lighter accent, but it has to be consistent.

Of her son Angela says, "He knows me well. If I start getting naughty he'll rap me on the knuckles."

Peter's function is more all-purpose. The retired M-G-M executive and former William Morris agent has managed his wife's career full time since 1973 and now acts as overseer on all aspects of production for "Murder, She Wrote." It is Peter who screens the dailies, makes suggestions, criticizes when necessary; and acts as Angela's "third eye."

"Peter works out every move in his head as if he were always playing a chess game," Angela reports admiringly. "I'm very levelheaded, but also very impulsive. In that sense, we balance each other nicely."

Peter also takes care of family affairs, makes sure the bills are paid, and even cooks dinner. When Angela comes home after a full day's shooting, that can sometimes be the biggest help of all.

The workload is horrendous. A single one-hour episode can take up to eight days to shoot. Portions of episodes can be shot on location anywhere from Seattle to Mendocino to New York to all over Southern California. A single day's shooting used to last up to sixteen hours, until Angela put her foot down.

"I won't work sixteen hours straight anymore," she says, having set her absolute cut-off time at twelve hours. "There is a limit to what you can do and still maintain your health. Saying 'no' has always been a problem for me. But I'm getting better at it."

Still, she managed to strain her back badly enough during one scene to land in bed, only because she insisted on attending the Golden Globe Awards the following night instead of staying home. She and "Murder, She Wrote" each won an award, but Angela was laid up for days.

"This is the first time this has happened to me," she lamented when it happened. "Honestly, I have never known such pain in my life. It's like giving birth at sixty! I had no idea how all-absorbing the work would be."

It is absorbing, of course, only to someone who takes herself and her work as seriously as Angela does. If some television studio insists on paying her upwards of $40,000 per week, she's going to see to it that they get their money's worth. She will also do everything she can to improve the overall quality of the product. Viewers have noticed a steady stream of well-known faces from Broadway and film. Anyone Angela has ever worked with before is automatically under consideration for casting. William Windom, Tom Bosley, Arthur Hill, Harry Guardino, Carol Lawrence, Ned Beatty, Jayne Meadows Allen, Robert Culp, Rex Smith, Robert Hooks—the list is virtually endless. Angela knows quality, and knows that surrounding Jessica Fletcher with such professionals can only make her look better.

Stories leak out once in a while: For example, that she never allows visitors on the set, and due to her gentle persuasion, the first season's thirteen directors were whittled down to five. Two stories in particular demonstrate Angela's singleminded dedication to the show. One has to do with a very young television actress, who shall remain nameless.

"There was one particular cute young actress who was having a devil of a time in a scene," Angela recollects. "She was supposed to break down in uncontrollable sobs during my questioning. But after eight takes, she still acted as though she was having a roaring good time instead of being distraught. Now, mind you, I've been acting longer than she's been living, so I just called for a break, took her aside and coached her with the scene."

By contrast, there was the time Lloyd Nolan appeared as a guest star. He was eighty-two and quite ill; "Murder, She Wrote" was to be the last work he did before his death. When he couldn't remember his lines, it was Angela who coached him, whispered his cues, held his hand, and nursed him through scenes, comforting him by saying, "Don't get upset, Lloyd. I blow lines, too." Watching the episode, it is imposible to tell how difficult it was.

Angela has reasons for every bit of input she provides. "I prefer directors with stage experience who know something about actors and acting and who don't make you feel like a piece of furniture to be moved around," she states. As for casting decisions: "I just want them to give me good actors to work with, no matter what their age or TVQ."

The impression that the lady calls the shots is probably accurate. And it works. "Murder, She Wrote" has won its Golden Globes, and is a consistent third place in the Nielsens this season. Angela is acknowledged as the most tuned-in female face on television. Only "Bill Cosby" and "Family Ties" give her any serious competition. Jessica Fletcher is even popular in Europe.

"People have a real affection for Jessica and they admire her," says her alter ego. "There are a lot of middle-aged women out there who are thrilled to see someone in their age bracket depicted in a positive, upbeat way."

The star herself may be less thrilled, if only because she doesn't see what all the fuss is about. Compared to some of the work she has had to do on stage and in film, Jessica Fletcher is child's play.

"When you're working on a series, there's no life outside it," Angela laments. "Which is pretty stupid when you stop and analyze what you're doing—just running down corridors and things, to which they seem to attach great importance. I sometimes feel I'm playing an older Nancy Drew."

Still, she can't resist adding her own little personal touches. One episode called for her to play a double role, as both Jessica and her cousin, a British music hall singer. The cousin was named Emma MacGill, in memory of Moyna.

The scriptwriter had not decided on a particular song for Emma to do as her opening number. Producer Peter Fischer sent to England for the sheet music to several dozen vintage music hall numbers, but Angela was one step ahead of him. She got on the phone with no less than Stephen Sondheim, seeking his advice. To her surprise he tapped into her pet fantasy, suggesting she sing "Goodbye, Little Yellow Bird" from *Dorian Gray*.

Forty-one years after she'd sung it first, the song that introduced her career was immortalized in the hearts of TV audiences on two continents.

Angela and Peter didn't buy their home in Brentwood until nearly six months after the Golden Globe Awards. Levelheaded Angela has been involved in too many "sure things" to trust something as tenuous as a television show.

Stepping over packing crates and topsy-turvy furniture for the umpteenth time in her life, wearing a T-shirt printed with "This Is No Ordinary Housewife," Angela has come home.

"We have a beautiful apartment on the forty-fourth floor of the Manhattan Plaza and a farmhouse in upstate New York," she says. "But until now we haven't really put our roots back down in the USA."

The house is beautiful. Modest by posh Brentwood standards, it has three bedrooms—for visiting children and grandchildren—tile floors, four fireplaces, skylights, and a pool. Angela's first obsession was to pore over gardening books and seed catalogues. She had returned to Hollywood the year before with nothing but three potted plants.

"My last great ambition in life is to create a garden from scratch," she says. "I want to prepare the soil and just watch my flowers grow. One of the problems in my business is that we are all gypsies. But stability is the thing I long for most."

"I think Angela will never again stop devoting herself to mother-henning her family," Peter says fondly. "After all, now we've got grandchildren to keep an eye on, too."

As for what's next on the creative horizon, only time will tell. Good friend Fritz Holt sees Jessica Fletcher as the best thing that could happen to Angela at this point in her career. "Jessica is close to Angela's roots. She's always had a yen for a sleuthy part. It's a well-earned respite from the theater. It's making her a worldwide name, and she'll bring that level of recognition with her when she returns to the stage."

There doesn't seem to be any question in anyone's mind that she *will* return to the stage.

"The great film or play for Mother hasn't been written yet," Anthony says. "I think she'll regroup after this TV experience and try to make sure it comes along."

While she waits for that golden opportunity, Angela refuses to sit still. In addition to her grueling schedule on "Murder, She Wrote," she manages to find time to do the occasional movie, such as *The Company Of Wolves.* A sort of post-Freudian variation on *Little Red Riding Hood,* this not-quite-horror film features Angela as the grandmother who turns her granddaughter's nightmares of wolves and spooky happenings into exotic psychology-laden fairy tales. For someone who began her career playing Little Red Riding Hood in a family Christmas pageant, *The Company Of Wolves* is another example of life coming full circle.

Now that the world's her oyster, what does Angela want to do most? She thinks about it for a long moment.

"I've done movies, drama, musicals, singing, dancing and now television. What haven't I done yet? Oh, yes, nobody has ever cast me in a Restoration comedy, which I always loved as a student.

"Suppose, just suppose, someone invited me to do Oliver Goldsmith's *She Stoops To Conquer?* I'd grab it in a minute!"

FILMOGRAPHY

Gaslight. Screenplay by John Van Druten, Walter Reisch, and John L. Balderston; based on the play by Patrick Hamilton; directed by George Cukor; produced by Arthur Hornblow Jr. for Metro-Goldwyn-Mayer. Released: May, 1944.

CAST

Gregory Anton . . . . . . Charles Boyer
Paula Alquist . . . . . . Ingrid Bergman
Brian Cameron . . . . . . Joseph Cotten
Miss Thwaites . . . . . . Dame May Whitty
Nancy . . . . . . *Angela Lansbury*
Elizabeth . . . . . Barbara Everest
Maestro Guardi . . . . . . Emil Rameau
General Huddleston . . . . . . Edmund Breon
Mr. Mufflin . . . . . . Halliwell Hobbes
Williams . . . . . . Tom Stevenson
Lady Dalroy . . . . . . Heather Thatcher
Lord Dalroy . . . . . . Lawrence Grossmith
Pianist . . . . . . Jakob Gimbel

National Velvet. Screenplay by Theodore Reeves and Helen Deutsch; based on the novel by Enid Bagnold; directed by Clarence Brown; produced by Pandro S. Berman for Metro-Goldwyn-Mayer. Released: December, 1944.

CAST

Mr. Taylor . . . . . . Mickey Rooney
Mr. Brown . . . . . . Donald Crisp
Velvet Brown . . . . . . Elizabeth Taylor
Mrs. Brown . . . . . . Anne Revere
Edwina Brown . . . . . . *Angela Lansbury*
Donald Brown . . . . . . Jackie Jenkins

173

```
             Marvolio Brown . . . . . . Juanita Quigley
              Race Patron . . . . . . Arthur Treacher
               Farmer Ede . . . . . Reginald Owen
                 Miss Sims . . . . . Norma Varden
                     Ted . . . . . Terry Kilburn
               Jockey Taski . . . . . . Eugene Loring
                  Hallam . . . . . Arthur Shields
```

The Picture Of Dorian Gray. Screenplay by Albert Lewin; based on the novel by Oscar Wilde; directed by Albert Lewin; cinematography by Harry Stradling; produced by Pandro S. Berman for Metro-Goldwyn-Mayer. Released: March, 1945.

CAST

```
          Lord Henry Wotton . . . . . . George Sanders
              Dorian Gray . . . . . . Hurd Hatfield
           Gladys Hallward . . . . . . Donna Reed
               Sybil Vane . . . . . . Angela Lansbury
              David Stone . . . . . . Peter Lawford
            Basil Hallward . . . . . . Lowell Gilmore
               James Vane . . . . . . Richard Fraser
            Allen Campbell . . . . . . Douglas Walton
           Adrian Singleton . . . . . . Morton Lowry
         Sir Robert Bentley . . . . . . Miles Mander
                Mrs. Vane . . . . . . Lydia Bilbrook
              Lady Agatha . . . . . . Mary Forbes
               Sir Thomas . . . . . . Robert Greig
                 Duchess . . . . . . Moyna MacGill
     Malvolio Jones Chairman . . . . . . Billy Bevan
       Young Frenchwoman . . . . . . Renee Carson
                   Kate . . . . . . Lillian Bond
```

The Harvey Girls. Screenplay by Edmund Beloin, Nathaniel Curtis, Harry Crane, James O'Hanlon, and Samson Raphaelson; additional dialogue by

Kay Van Riper; based on the book by Samuel Hopkins Adams; words and music by Johnny Mercer and Harry Warren. Directed by George Sidney; produced by Arthur Freed for Metro-Goldwyn-Mayer. Released: January, 1946.

CAST

Judy Garland
John Hodiak
Ray Bolger
Angela Lansbury
Preston Foster
Virginia O'Brien
Kenny Baker
Marjorie Main
Chill Wills
Selena Royle
Cyd Charisse
Ruth Brady
Jack Lambert
Edward Earle
Morris Ankrum
William "Bill" Phillips
Ben Carter
Norman Leavitt
Horace McNally

The Hoodlum Saint. Original screenplay by Frank Wead and James Hill; directed by Norman Taurog; produced by Cliff Reid for Metro-Goldwyn-Mayer. Released: June, 1946.

CAST

Terry Ellerton O'Neill . . . . . . William Powell
Kay Lorrison . . . . . . Esther Williams
Dusty Millard . . . . . . *Angela Lansbury*
Snarp . . . . . . James Gleason

Father Nolan . . . . . Lewis Stone
Fishface . . . . . . Rags Ragland
Three Finger . . . . . . Frank McHugh
Eel . . . . . Slim Summerville
Father O'Doul . . . . . Roman Bohnen
Uncle Joe Lorrison . . . . . . Charles Trowbridge
Lewis J. Malbery . . . . . . Henry O'Neill
Dave Fernby . . . . . . William Phillips
Father Duffy . . . . . . Matt Moore
Rabbi Meyerberg . . . . . Trevor Bardette
Reverend Miller . . . . . . Addison Richards
Maggie . . . . . . Emma Dunn
Trina . . . . . . Mary Gordon

Till The Clouds Roll By. Screenplay by Myles Connolly and Jean Holloway, adapted by George Wells from a story by Guy Bolton; directed by Richard Whorf; musical numbers staged and directed by Robert Alton; music by Jerome Kern; produced by Arthur Freed for Metro-Goldwyn-Mayer. Released: December, 1946.

CAST

Jerome Kern . . . . . . Robert Walker
Marilyn Miller . . . . . . Judy Garland
Sally . . . . . . Lucille Bremer
Sally as a girl . . . . . . Joan Wells
James I. Hessler . . . . . . Van Heflin
Oscar Hammerstein . . . . . . Paul Langton
Mrs. Jerome Kern . . . . . . Dorothy Patrick
Mrs. Muller . . . . . . Mary Nash
Charles Frohman . . . . . . Harry Hayden
Victor Herbert . . . . . Paul Maxey
Cecil Keller . . . . . . Rex Evans
Hennessey . . . . . William Phillips
Julia Sanderson . . . . . Dinah Shore
Band Leader . . . . . . Van Johnson

With: June Allyson, *Angela Lansbury,* Ray McDonald, Kathryn Grayson, Frank Sinatra, Virginia O'Brien, Lena Horne, Tony Martin, William Halligan, Caleb Peterson, Bruce Cowling, Maurice Kelly, Cyd Charisse, Gower Champion, Ray Teal, the Wilde Twins, Byron Foulger.

The Private Affairs of Bel Ami. Screenplay by Albert Lewin; based on the novel by Guy de Maupassant; directed by Albert Lewin; produced by David L. Loew for United Artists. Released: June, 1947.

CAST

George Duroy (Bel Ami) . . . . . . George Sanders
Madeleine Forestier . . . . . . Ann Dvorak
Gintilde de Marelle . . . . . . *Angela Lansbury*
Marie de Varenne . . . . . . Frances Dee
Charles Forestier . . . . . . John Carradine
Suzanne Walter . . . . . . Susan Douglas
Monsieur Walter . . . . . . Hugo Hass
Madame Walter . . . . . . Katherine Emery
Rachel Michot . . . . . . Marie Wilson
Jacques Rival . . . . . . Albert Basserman
Laroche-Mathieu . . . . . . Warren William
Philippe de Cantel . . . . . . Richard Fraser

Tenth Avenue Angel. Screenplay by Harry Ruskin and Eleanore Griffen, based on a story by Angna Enders and a sketch by Craig Rice; directed by Roy Rowland; produced by Ralph Wheelwright for Metro-Goldwyn-Mayer. Released: 1947.

CAST

George Murphy
Warner Anderson
Phyllis Thaxter
Margaret O'Brien

Angela Lansbury
Barry Nelson
Rhys Williams
Connie Gilchrist
Tom Trout
Audrey Totter

If Winter Comes. Screenplay by Marguerite Roberts and Arthur Wimperls, based on the novel by A.S.M. Hutchinson; directed by Victor Saville; produced by Pandro S. Berman for Metro-Goldwyn-Mayer. Released: January, 1948.

CAST

Mark Sabre	Walter Pidgeon
Nina Tybar	Deborah Kerr
Mabel Sabre	*Angela Lansbury*
Natalie Bagshaw	Binnie Barnes
Effie Bright	Janet Leigh
Mrs. Perch	Dame May Whitty
Sarah "Low Jinks"	Rene Ray
Rebecca "High Jinks"	Virginia Kelley
Mr. Fortune	Reginald Owen
Mr. Twyning	John Abbott
Mr. Bright	Rhys Williams
Tony Tybar	Hugh French
Tony Wilson	Dennis Hoey
Mr. Pettigrew	Nicholas Joy
The Coroner	Halliwell Hobbes
Mr. Fergus	Victor Wood
Freddie Perch	Hugh Green
Harold Twyning	James Wethered
"Uncle" Fouraker	Owen McGiveney

State Of The Union. Screenplay by Anthony Veiller and Myles Connolly, based on the play by Howard Lindsay and Russell Crouse; directed and produced by Frank Capra for Liberty Films and released by Metro-Goldwyn-Mayer: April, 1948.

CAST

Grant Matthews . . . . . . Spencer Tracy
Mary Matthews . . . . . . Katharine Hepburn
"Spike" McManus . . . . . . Van Johnson
Kay Thorndyke . . . . . . *Angela Lansbury*
Jim Conover . . . . . . Adolphe Menjou
Sam Thorndyke . . . . . Lewis Stone
Sam I. Parrish . . . . . . Howard Smith
Bill Hardy . . . . . . Charles Dingle
Lulubelle Alexander . . . . . . Maidel Turner
Judge Alexander . . . . . . Raymond Walburn
Norah . . . . . . Margaret Hamilton
Radio Announcer . . . . . . Art Baker
Senator Lauterback . . . . . . Pierre Watkin
Grace Orval Draper . . . . . . Florence Auer
Buck Swenson . . . . . . Irving Bacon
Blink Moran . . . . . . Charles Lane
Joyce Matthews . . . . . . Patti Brady
Grant Matthews Jr. . . . . . . George Nokes
Bellboy . . . . . Carl "Alfalfa" Switzer
Waiter . . . . . . Tom Fadden
Barber . . . . . . Tom Pedi

The Three Musketeers. Screenplay by Robert Ardrey, based on the novel by Alexandre Dumas; directed by George Sidney; produced by Pandro S. Berman for Metro-Goldwyn-Mayer. Released: October, 1948.

CAST

Lady de Winter . . . . . . Lana Turner
D'Artagnan . . . . . . Gene Kelly
Constance . . . . . . June Allyson
Athos . . . . . . Van Heflin

Queen Anne . . . . . . *Angela Lansbury*
King Louis XIII . . . . . Frank Morgan
Richelieu . . . . . Vincent Price
Planchet . . . . . Keenan Wynn
Duke of Buckingham . . . . . John Sutton
Porthos . . . . . Gig Young
Aramis . . . . . Robert Coote
Treville . . . . . Reginald Owen
Rochefort . . . . . Ian Keith
Kitty . . . . . Patricia Medina
Albert . . . . . Richard Stapley

Samson And Delilah. Screenplay by Jesse L. Lasky Jr. and Frederic M. Franc, from original treatments by Harold Lamb and Vladimir Jabotinsky; produced and directed by Cecil B. DeMille for Paramount Pictures. Released: December, 1949.

CAST

Delilah . . . . . Hedy Lamarr
Samson . . . . . Victor Mature
The Saran of Gaza . . . . . George Sanders
Semader . . . . . *Angela Lansbury*
Ahtur . . . . . Henry Wilcoxon
Miriam . . . . . Olive Dearing
Hazelelponit . . . . . Fay Holden
Hisham . . . . . Julia Faye
Saul . . . . . Rusty Tamblyn
Tubal . . . . . William Farnum
Teresh . . . . . Lane Chandler
Targil . . . . . Moroni Olsen
Story Teller . . . . . Francis J. McDonald
Garmiskar . . . . . William Davis
Leah Lakish . . . . . John Miljan

The Red Danube. Screenplay by Gina Kaus and Arthur Wimperls, based on the novel *Vespers In Vienna* by Bruce Marshall; directed by George Sidney;

produced by Carey Wilson for Metro-Goldwyn-Mayer. Released: December, 1949.

CAST

Col. Michael "Hooky" Nicobar . . . . . . Walter Pidgeon
The Mother Superior . . . . . Ethel Barrymore
Major John "Twingo" McPhimister . . . . . Peter Lawford
Audrey Quail . . . . . . *Angela Lansbury*
Maria Buhlen . . . . . . Janet Leigh
Col. Piniev . . . . . . Louis Calhern
Col. Humphrey "Blinker" Omicron . . . . . Francis L. Sullivan
Private David Moonlight . . . . . . Melville Cooper
Brig. C.M.V. Catlock . . . . . . Robert Coote
The General . . . . . . Alan Napier
2nd Lt. Maxim Omansky . . . . . . Roman Toporov
Sister Kasimira . . . . . . Kasla Orzazewski
Helena Nagard . . . . . Tamara Shayne
Prof. Serge Bruloff . . . . . . Konstantin Shayne
"Mickey Mouse" . . . . . . Janine Perreau
Lt. Guedalia-Wood . . . . . David Hydes

Kind Lady. Screenplay by Jerry Davis, Edward Chodorov, and Charles Bennett; adapted from the play by Edward Chodorov and the story by Hugh Walpole; directed by John Sturges; produced by Armand Deutsch for Metro-Goldwyn-Mayer. Released: August, 1951.

CAST

Mary Herries . . . . . . Ethel Barrymore
Henry Springer Elcott . . . . . Maurice Evans
Mrs. Edwards . . . . . . *Angela Lansbury*
Edwards . . . . . Keenan Wynn
Ada Elcott . . . . . . Betsy Blair
Mr. Foster . . . . . . John Williams
Rose . . . . . Doris Lloyd
Antique Dealer . . . . . . John O'Malley
Monsieur Malaquaise . . . . . . Henri Letondal

Mrs. Markley	. . . . . .	Moyna MacGill
Mr. Markley	. . . . . .	Barry Bernard
Lucy Weston	. . . . . .	Sally Cooper
Chauffeur	. . . . . .	Arthur Gould-Porter
Aggie Edwards	. . . . . .	Sherlee Collier
Dora	. . . . . .	Phyllis Morris
Constable Orkin	. . . . . .	Patrick O'Moore
Jones	. . . . . .	Keith McConnell
Postman	. . . . . .	Leonard Carey
Doc	. . . . . .	Victor Wood

Mutiny. Based on the novel *The Golden Anchor* by Hollister Noble. A United Artists release: 1952.

CAST

Mark Stevens
Patric Knowles
Angela Lansbury
Gene Evans
Rhys Williams
Robert Osterloh
Peter Brocco
Norman Leavitt
Gene Roth
Walter Sande
Clayton Moore
Morris Ankrum
Todd Karnes
Louis Jean Heydt
Robin Hughes
Crane Whitley

Remains To Be Seen. Screenplay by Sidney Sheldon, based on the play by Howard Lindsay and Russell Crouse; directed by Don Weiss; produced by Arthur Hornblow for Metro-Goldwyn-Mayer. Released: 1953.

CAST

June Allyson
Van Johnson
Dorothy Dandridge
Angela Lansbury
Louis Calhern
John Beal
Barry Kelley
Sammy White
Kathryn Card
Helene Millard
Paul Harvey
Morgan Farley
Howard Freeman

Key Man. (Released in England as *A Life At Stake*). A filmakers/Gibraltar Motion Picture Distributors release: April, 1955. Costarring Keith Andes and *Angela Lansbury.*

The Purple Mask. Screenplay by Oscar Brodney, from a play by Paul Armont and Jean Manoussi; directed by Bruce Humberstone; produced by Howard Christie for Universal-International. Released: June, 1955.

CAST

Rene . . . . . . Tony Curtis
Laurette . . . . . . Colleen Miller
Laverne . . . . . . Gene Barry
Brisquet . . . . . . Dan O'Herlihy
Madame Valentine . . . . . . *Angela Lansbury*
Cadonal . . . . . . George Dolenz
Fouche . . . . . . John Hoyt
Constance . . . . . . Myrna Hansen
Duce DeLatour . . . . . . Paul Cavanaugh
Napoleon . . . . . . Robert Cornthwaite

A Lawless Street. Based on the novel *The Marshall of Medicine Bend* by Brad Ward; produced by Harry Joe Brown for Columbia Pictures. Released: December, 1955.

CAST

Calem Ware . . . . . . Randolph Scott
Tally Dickinson . . . . . . *Angela Lansbury*
Homer Thorne . . . . . . Warner Anderson
Cora Dean . . . . . . Jean Parker
Dr. Amos Wynn . . . . . . Wallace Ford
Cody Clark . . . . . . John Emery
Asaph Dean . . . . . . James Bell
Molly Higgins . . . . . . Ruth Donnelly
Harley Baskam . . . . . . Michael Pate
Dooley Brion . . . . . . Don Megowan
Mrs. Dingo Brion . . . . . . Jeanette Nolan
Hiram Hayes . . . . . . Peter Ortiz
Juan Tobrez . . . . . . Don Carlos
Dingo Brion . . . . . . Frank Hagney
Willis . . . . . . Charles Williams
Abe Deland . . . . . . Frank Ferguson
Tony Cabrillo . . . . . . Harry Tyler
Major Kent . . . . . . Harry Antrim

The Court Jester. Written, produced, and directed by Norman Panama and Melvin Frank for Paramount Pictures, words and music by Sylvia Fine and Sammy Kahn. Released: February, 1956.

CAST

Hawkins . . . . . . Danny Kaye
Maid Jean . . . . . . Glynis Johns
Sir Ravenhurst . . . . . . Basil Rathbone
Princess Gwendolyn . . . . . . *Angela Lansbury*
King Roderick . . . . . . Cecil Parker
Griselda . . . . . . Mildred Natwick

Sir Griswold . . . . . Robert Middleton
Sir Locksley . . . . . . Michael Pate
Captain of the Guard . . . . . Herbert Rudley
Fergus . . . . . . Noel Drayton
Black Fox . . . . . . Edward Ashley
Giacomo . . . . . . John Carradine
Sir Brockhurst . . . . . . Alan Napier
Sir Rinsdale . . . . . . Lewis Martin
Sir Pertwee . . . . . . Patrick Aherne
Archbishop . . . . . . Richard Kean
and Hermine's Midgets

Please Murder Me. From an original screenplay; a Distributors Corporation of America release: March, 1956.

CAST

Angela Lansbury
Raymond Burr
Dick Foran
John Dehner
Lamont Johnson
Robert Griffin
Denver Pyle
Alex Sharpe
Lee Miller
Madge Blake
Russ Thorson

The Long, Hot Summer. Screenplay by Irving Ravetch and Harriet Frank Jr., based on *The Hamlet* and other stories by William Faulkner; directed by Martin Ritt; produced by Jerry Wald; presented by Twentieth-Century Fox. Released: April, 1958.

185

CAST

Ben Quick . . . . . Paul Newman
Clara Varner . . . . . Joanne Woodward
Jody . . . . . Anthony Franciosa
Varner . . . . . Orson Welles
Eula Varner . . . . . Lee Remick
Minnie . . . . . *Angela Lansbury*
Alan Stewart . . . . . Richard Anderson
Agnes Stewart . . . . . Sarah Marshall
Mrs. Stewart . . . . . Mabel Albertson
Ratliff . . . . . J. Pat O'Malley
Lucius . . . . . William Walker
Peabody . . . . . George Dunn
Armstead . . . . . Jess Kirkpatrick
Wilk . . . . . Val Avery
Houstin . . . . . I. Stanford Jolley
John Fisher . . . . . Nicholas King
Tom Shortly . . . . . Leif Erickson
J.V. Brokright . . . . . Ralph Reed

The Reluctant Debutante. Screenplay by William Douglas Home, based on his play of the same name; directed by Vincente Minnelli; produced by Pandro S. Berman; an Avon Production released by Metro-Goldwyn-Mayer: August, 1958.

CAST

Lord Jimmy Broadbent . . . . . . Rex Harrison
Lady Sheila Broadbent . . . . . Kay Kendall
David Parkson . . . . . John Saxon
Jane Broadbent . . . . . Sandra Dee
Mabel Claremont . . . . . . *Angela Lansbury*
David Fenner . . . . . Peter Myers
Clarissa Claremont . . . . . Diane Clare

The Dark At The Top Of The Stairs. Screenplay by Harriet Frank Jr. and Irving Ravetch, based on the play by William Inge; directed by Delbert Mann; produced by Michael Garrison for Warner Brothers. Released: September, 1960.

CAST

Rubin Flood . . . . . . Robert Preston
Cora Flood . . . . . . Dorothy McGuire
Reenie Flood . . . . . . Shirley Knight
Sonny Flood . . . . . . Robert Eyer
Lottie . . . . . . Eve Arden
Mavis . . . . . . *Angela Lansbury*
Sammy Golden . . . . . . Lee Kinsolving
Morris . . . . . . Frank Overton
Flirt . . . . . . Penney Parker
Ken Lynch . . . . . . Harry Ralston

A Breath Of Scandal. Screenplay by Walter Bernstein, based on the play *Olympia* by Ferenc Molnar; directed by Michael Curtiz; produced by Carlo Ponti and Morcello Girosi; released by Paramount Pictures: December, 1960.

CAST

Olympia . . . . . . Sophia Loren
Charlie . . . . . . John Gavin
Philip . . . . . . Maurice Chevalier
Eugenie . . . . . . Isabel Jeans
Lina . . . . . . *Angela Lansbury*
Albert . . . . . . Tullio Carminati
Aide . . . . . . Robert Risso
Rupert . . . . . . Carlo Hintermann
Can-Can Girl . . . . . . Milly Vitale
Count Sandor . . . . . . Frederick Ledebur

Season of Passion. (British release title: *Summer Of The Seventeenth Doll*) Based on the novel of the same name by Ray Lawler; a United Artists release: October, 1961.

CAST

Roo . . . . . . Ernest Borgnine
Olive . . . . . . Anne Baxter
Barney . . . . . . John Mills
Pearl . . . . . . *Angela Lansbury*
Dowd . . . . . . Vincent Ball
Emma . . . . . . Ethel Gabriel
Bubba . . . . . . Janette Craig
Spruiker . . . . . . Deryck Barnes
"The Atomic Bomber" . . . . . . Tom Lurich
Cane Cutters . . . . . . Al Thomas
Al Garcia
Frank Wilson
Little Girl . . . . . . Dana Wilson
Nancy . . . . . . Jessica Noad

Blue Hawaii. Screenplay by Hal Kanter; directed by Norman Taurog; produced by Hal Wallis for Paramount Pictures. Released: February, 1962.

CAST

Chad Gates . . . . . . Elvis Presley
Maile Duval . . . . . . Joan Blackman
Miss Prentice . . . . . . Nancy Walters
Mr. Gates . . . . . . Roland Winters
Mrs. Gates . . . . . . *Angela Lansbury*
Jack Kelman . . . . . . John Archer
Ellie . . . . . . Jenny Maxwell
Mr. Chapman . . . . . . Howard McNear
Patsy . . . . . . Darlene Tompkins
Sandy . . . . . . Pamela Akert

All Fall Down. Screenplay by William Inge, from the novel by James Leo Herlihy; directed by John Frankenheimer; produced by John Houseman for Metro-Goldwyn-Mayer. Released: April, 1962.

CAST

Echo O'Brien . . . . . . Eva Marie Saint
Berry-Berry Willart . . . . . Warren Beatty
Ralph Willart . . . . . . Karl Malden
Annabel Willart . . . . . . *Angela Lansbury*
Clinton Willart . . . . . . Brandon De Wilde
Mrs. Mandel . . . . . . Constance Ford
Schoolteacher . . . . . . Barbara Baxley
Hedy . . . . . . Evans Evans
Myra . . . . . Jennifer Howard
Bouncer . . . . . Madame Spivy

The Manchurian Candidate. Screenplay by George Axelrod, based on the novel by Richard Condon; directed by John Frankenheimer; produced by George Axelrod and John Frankenheimer; released by United Artists: October, 1962.

CAST

Bennett Marco . . . . . . Frank Sinatra
Raymond Shaw . . . . . . Laurence Harvey
Rosie . . . . . Janet Leigh
Raymond's Mother . . . . . . *Angela Lansbury*
Chunjin . . . . . . Henry Silva
Senator Iselin . . . . . . James Gregory
Jocie Jordan . . . . . . Leslie Parrish
Senator Jordan . . . . . . John McGiver
Yen Lo . . . . . Khigh Dhiegh
Corporal Melvin . . . . . James Edwards
Colonel . . . . . . Douglas Henderson
Zilkov . . . . . . Albert Paulsen
Secretary of Defense . . . . . Barry Kelley

Holborn Gaines . . . . . . Lloyd Corrigan
Berezovo . . . . . . Madame Spivy

In The Cool Of The Day. Screenplay by Meade Roberts, based on the novel by Susan Ertz; directed by Robert Stevens; produced by John Houseman for Metro-Goldwyn-Mayer. Released: May, 1963.

CAST

Murray Logan . . . . . . Peter Finch
Christine Bonner . . . . . . Jane Fonda
Sibyl Logan . . . . . . Angela Lansbury
Sam Bonner . . . . . . Arthur Hill
Mrs. Gellert . . . . . . Constance Cummings
Frederick Bonner . . . . . . Alexander Knox

The World Of Henry Orient. Screenplay by Nora and Nunnally Johnson, based on a novel by Nora Johnson; directed by George Roy Hill; produced by Jerome Hellman; a Pan Arts Company presentation released through United Artists: March, 1964.

CAST

Henry Orient . . . . . . Peter Sellers
Stella . . . . . . Paula Prentiss
Valerie Boyd . . . . . . Tippy Walker
Marian Gilbert . . . . . . Merrie Spaeth
Isabel Boyd . . . . . . Angela Lansbury
Frank Boyd . . . . . . Tom Bosley
Mrs. Gilbert . . . . . . Phyllis Thaxter
Boothy . . . . . . Bibi Osterwald
Joe Byrd . . . . . . Peter Duchin
Sidney . . . . . . John Fiedler
The Store Owner . . . . . . Al Lewis
The Doctor . . . . . . Fred Stewart

190

Emma . . . . . . Philippa Bevans
Katritz . . . . . . Jane Buchanan

Dear Heart. Screenplay by Tad Mosel from his story; directed by Delbert Mann; produced by Martin Manulis; a Warner Brothers release: March, 1965.

CAST

Harry Mork . . . . . . Glenn Ford
Evie Jackson . . . . . . Geraldine Page
Phyllis . . . . . . Angela Lansbury
Patrick . . . . . . Michael Anderson Jr.
June . . . . . . Barbara Nichols
Mitchell . . . . . . Patricia Barry
Frank Taylor . . . . . . Charles Drake
Miss Tait . . . . . . Ruth McDevitt
Connie . . . . . . Neva Patterson
Miss Moore . . . . . . Alice Pearce
Mr. Cruikshank . . . . . . Richard Deacon
Zola . . . . . . Joanna Crawford
Peterson . . . . . . Peter Turgeon
The Masher . . . . . . Ken Lynch

The Amorous Adventures Of Moll Flanders. Screenplay by Dennis Cannan and Roland Kibbee, based on the book by Daniel Defoe; directed by Terence Young; produced by Marcel Hellman for Paramount Pictures. Released: May, 1965.

CAST

Moll Flanders . . . . . . Kim Novak
Jemmy . . . . . . Richard Johnson
Lady Blystone . . . . . . Angela Lansbury
Dutchy . . . . . . Lilli Palmer

```
William . . . . . . George Sanders
Squint . . . . . . Leo McKern
The Count . . . . . Vittorio De Sica
The Elder Brother . . . . . Daniel Massey
The Younger Brother . . . . . Derren Nesbitt
The Mayor . . . . . . Cecil Parker
```

Harlow. Screenplay by John Michael Hayes, based on the book by Irving Shulman; directed by Gordon Douglas; produced by Joseph E. Levine for Paramount Pictures. Released: July, 1965.

CAST

```
Jean Harlow . . . . . . Carroll Baker
Arthur Landau . . . . . . Red Buttons
Jack Harrison . . . . . . Michael Connors
Paul Bern . . . . . . Peter Lawford
Everett Redman . . . . . . Martin Balsam
Mama Jean Bello . . . . . . Angela Lansbury
Marino Bello . . . . . . Raf Vallone
Richard Manley . . . . . . Leslie Nielsen
Mrs. Landau . . . . . . Hanna Landy
Assistant Director . . . . . . Peter Hansen
```

The Greatest Story Ever Told. Screenplay by George Stevens and James Lee Barrett, from a book by Fulton Oursler, the writings of Henry Denker and the Bible; produced and directed by George Stevens for United Artists. Released: 1965.

CAST

```
Jesus Christ . . . . . . Max von Sydow
John the Baptist . . . . . . Charlton Heston
Virgin Mary . . . . . . Dorothy McGuire
James the Younger . . . . . . Michael Anderson Jr.
```

Angel at the Tomb . . . . . . Pat Boone
Herod Antipas . . . . . . Jose Ferrer
Barabbas . . . . . . Richard Conte
Sorak . . . . . . Victor Buono
Philip . . . . . . David Hedison
Caiaphas . . . . . . Martin Landau
Claudia . . . . . . Angela Lansbury
Joseph . . . . . . Robert Loggia
Bar Amand . . . . . . Van Heflin
Mary of Bethany . . . . . . Janet Margolin
Judas Iscariot . . . . . . David McCallum
Matthew . . . . . . Roddy McDowall
Uriah . . . . . . Sal Mineo
Herod . . . . . . Claude Rains
Old Aram . . . . . . Ed Wynn
Woman of No Name . . . . . . Shelley Winters
Pontius Pilate . . . . . . Telly Savalas
Simon of Cyrene . . . . . . Sidney Poitier
Shemiah . . . . . . Nehemiah Persoff
The Dark Hermit/Satan . . . . . . Donald Pleasance
Roman Centurion . . . . . . John Wayne
Veronica . . . . . . Carroll Baker
Simon the Zealot . . . . . . Robert Blake
Andrew . . . . . . Burt Brinckerhoff
John . . . . . . John Considine
Thaddeus . . . . . . Jamie Farr
Nathanael . . . . . . Peter Mann
Peter . . . . . . Gary Raymond
Thomas . . . . . . Tom Reese
James the Elder . . . . . . David Sheiner
Martha of Bethany . . . . . . Ina Balin
Lazarus . . . . . . Michael Tolan
Mary Magdalene . . . . . . Joanna Dunham
Nicodemus . . . . . . Joseph Schildkraut
Questor . . . . . . Paul Stewart
Pilate's Aide . . . . . . Johnny Seven
General Varus . . . . . . Harold J. Stone
Emissary . . . . . . Robert Busch

Alexander . . . . . . John Crawford
Scribe . . . . . Russell Johnson
Speaker of Capernaum . . . . . John Lupton
Joseph of Arimathea . . . . . Abraham Sofaer
Theophilus . . . . . . Chet Stratton
Annas . . . . . . Ron Whelan
Aben . . . . . . John Abbott
Lancer Captain . . . . . . Rodolfo Acosta
Herod's Commander . . . . . . Michael Ansara
Chuza . . . . . . Philip Coolidge
Philip . . . . . . Dal Jenkins
Archelaus . . . . . . Joe Perry
Herodias . . . . . . Marian Seldes
Tormenter . . . . . . Frank De Kova
Dumah . . . . . . Joseph Sirola
Melchior . . . . . . Cyril Delvanti
Caspar . . . . . . Frank Silvera
Peter's Second Accuser . . . . . . John Pickard
Woman Behind Railings . . . . . . Celia Lovsky
Rabble Rouser . . . . . . Mickey Simpson
Good Thief . . . . . . Richard Bakalyan
Bad Thief . . . . . . Marc Cavell
Weeping Woman . . . . . . Renata Vanni

With: Frank Richards, Harry Wilson, Dorothy Neumann, and the Inbal Dance Theatre of Israel.

Mister Buddwing. (Original title: *Woman Without a Face*) Screenplay by Dale Wasserman, based on the novel *Buddwing* by Evan Hunter; directed by Delbert Mann; produced by Douglas Laurence and Delbert Mann; a DDD-Cherokee Production presented by Metro-Goldwyn-Mayer. Released: October, 1966.

CAST

Mister Buddwing . . . . . . James Garner
The Blonde . . . . . . Jean Simmons

```
        Fiddle . . . . . . Suzanne Pleshette
        Janet . . . . . . Katharine Ross
        Gloria . . . . . . Angela Lansbury
  Shabby Old Man . . . . . George Voskovec
     Mr. Schwartz . . . . . . Jack Gilford
   First Cab Driver . . . . . Joe Mantell
        Hank . . . . . . Raymond St. Jacques
         Dan . . . . . . Ken Lynch
     Policeman . . . . . . Beeson Carroll
  Second Cab Driver . . . . . . Billy Halop
    Counterman . . . . . . Michael Hadge
       Printer . . . . . . Charles Seal
        Tony . . . . . . John Tracy
      Chauffeur . . . . . . Bart Conrad
```

With: Wesley Addy, Romo Vincent, Nichelle Nichols, John Dennis, Kam Tong, James O'Rear, Rafael Campos and Rikki Stevens.

Something For Everyone. (released in Great Britain as Black Flowers For The Bride) Screenplay by Hugh Wheeler, based on a novel by Harry Kressing; directed by Harold Prince; cinematography by Walter Lassally; music by John Kander; produced by John P. Flaxman; released by National General Pictures: July, 1970.

CAST

```
Countess Herthe von Ornstein . . . . . . Angela Lansbury
     Conrad Ludwig . . . . . . Michael York
  Helmuth von Ornstein . . . . . . Anthony Corlan
  Annaliese von Ornstein . . . . . . Heidelinde Weis
      Mrs. Pleschke . . . . . . Eva-Marie Meineke
       Mr. Pleschke . . . . . . John Gill
    Lotte von Ornstein . . . . . . Jane Carr
        Bobby . . . . . . Despo
        Klaus . . . . . . Wilfrid Lier
     Father Georg . . . . . . Walter Janssen
       Rudolph . . . . . . Klaus Havenstein
```

Bedknobs And Broomsticks. Screenplay by Bill Walsh and Don DaGraul, based on a book by Mary Norton; directed by Robert Stevenson; produced by Bill Walsh; director of photography, Frank Phillips; music and lyrics by Richard M. Sherman and Robert B. Sherman; editor, Colton Warburton; a Walt Disney production for release by Buena Vista: November, 1971.

CAST

Miss Price	*Angela Lansbury*
Emilius	David Tomlinson
Mr. Jelk	Roddy MacDowall
Bookman	Sam Jaffe
Carrie	Cindy O'Callaghan
Paul	Roy Snart
Charlie	Ian Weighill
Col. Heller	John Ericson
Gen. Teagler	Reginald Owen
Mrs. Hobday	Tessie O'Shea

Death On The Nile. Based on the novel of the same title by Agatha Christie. An EMI/Paramount Pictures release: 1978.

CAST

Peter Ustinov
Jan Birken
Lois Chiles
Bette Davis
Mia Farrow
David Niven
Olivia Hussey
Angela Lansbury
Jack Warden
Maggie Smith

The Lady Vanishes. A Group Run Film, released in London: May, 1979.

CAST

Miss Froy . . . . . . *Angela Lansbury*
Amanda . . . . . . Cybill Shepherd
Comdon . . . . . . Elliott Gould

The Mirror Crack'd. Screenplay by Jonathan Hales and Barry Sandler; directed by Guy Hamilton; director of photography, Christopher Challis; film editor, Richard Marden; music by John Cameron; produced by John Brabourne and Richard Goodwin; distributed by EMI Films Ltd.; released by Associated Film Distribution. Released: December, 1980.

CAST

Miss Marple . . . . . . *Angela Lansbury*
Cherry . . . . . . Wendy Morgan
Mrs. Bantry . . . . . . Margaret Courtney
Bates . . . . . . Charles Gray
Heather Babcock . . . . . . Maureen Bennett
Miss Giles . . . . . . Carolyn Pickles
Major . . . . . . Eric Dodson
Vicar . . . . . . Charles Lloyd-Pack
Dr. Haydock . . . . . . Richard Pearson
Mayor . . . . . . Thick Wilson
Mayoress . . . . . . Pat Nye
Scout Master . . . . . . Peter Woodthorpe
Ella Zielinsky . . . . . . Geraldine Chaplin
Marty N. Fann . . . . . . Tony Curtis
Inspector Craddock . . . . . . Edward Fox
Jason Rudd . . . . . . Rock Hudson
Lola Brewster . . . . . . Kim Novak
Marina Rudd . . . . . . Elizabeth Taylor
Margot Bence . . . . . . Marelia Oppenheim

The Last Unicorn. An animated film directed and produced by Arthur Rankin, Jr. and Jules Bass; screenplay by Peter S. Beagle, based on his novel; camera by Hiroyasu Omoto; animations by Yoshiko Sasaki, Masahiro Yoshida, Kayoko Sakano, and Fukuo Suzuki; editor, Tornoko Kida. Music by Jimmy Webb. Lord Grade presents a Rankin/Bass production in association with ITC films. Released: November, 1982.

CAST

Schmendrick the Magician . . . . . . Alan Arkin
Prince Lir . . . . . . Jeff Bridges
The Last Unicorn/Lady Amalthea . . . . . . Mia Farrow
Molly Grue . . . . . . Tammy Grimes
The Butterfly . . . . . . Robert Klein
Mommy Fortuna . . . . . . Angela Lansbury
King Haggard . . . . . . Christopher Lee
Captain Cully . . . . . . Keenan Wynn
The Talking Cat . . . . . . Paul Frees
The Speaking Skull . . . . . . Rene Auberjonois

The Pirates of Penzance. A Universal Pictures release of a Joseph Papp production. Executive producer, Edward R. Pressman; producer, Joseph Papp; director, Wilford Leach. Screenplay by Wilford Leach, based on the operetta by W.S. Gilbert and A.S. Sullivan. Director of photography, Douglas Slocombe; additional photography by Paul Beeson; edited by Anne V. Coates. Music, Sir Arthur Seymour Sullivan; lyrics by William Schwenck Gilbert; additional music by William Elliott from themes by Arthur Sullivan. Released: February, 1983.

CAST

Pirate King . . . . . . Kevin Kline
Ruth . . . . . . Angela Lansbury
Mabel Stanley . . . . . . Linda Ronstadt
Major-General Stanley . . . . . . George Rose
Frederic . . . . . . Rex Smith

Sergeant . . . . . Tony Azito
Samuel . . . . . David Hatton
(sung by Stephen Hanon)
Edith . . . . . Louise Gold
(sung by Alexandra Korey)
Kate . . . . . Teresa Codling
(sung by Marcie Shaw)
Pinafore Company Orchestra Conductor . . . . . Preston Lockwood
Pinafore Captain . . . . . Romolo Bruni

PIRATES: Anthony Arundel, John Asquith, Mohamed Aazi, Tim Bentinck, Ross Davidson, Mike Grady, Sam Howe, Tony Millan, G.B. Zoot Money, Andrew Paul, Ken Leigh Rogers, Mohamed Serhani, Mike Walling.

DAUGHTERS: Leni Harper, Clare McIntyre, Louise Papillon, Tilly Vosburgh, Nancy Wood.

POLICEMEN: Peppi Borza, Nicolas Chagrin, Frankie Cull, David Hampshire, Phillip Harrison, Maurice Lane, Neil McCaul, Jerry Manley, Rhys Nelson, Garry Noakes, Chris Power, Kenny Warwick.

Pinafore Company: John Bett, Lennie Byrne, Jo MacReady, Brian Markham, Valerie Minifie, Linda Spurrier, Ursula Stedman.

The Company Of Wolves. Directed by Neil Jordan. Released: 1985.

CAST

Angela Lansbury
David Warner
Sarah Patterson
Micha Bergese

THEATER

Hotel Paradiso. A farce in three acts adapted by Peter Glenville from the French of Georges Feydeau and Maurice Desvallieres. Staged by Peter Glenville; settings and costumes by Osbert Lancaster; presented by Richard Myers, Julius Fleischmann, Charles Bowden, Richard Barr, and H. Ridgely Bullock Jr.; associate producer, Will Lester Productions; attraction supervised by Charles Lisanby and produced by arrangement with Hardy W. Smith and H.M. Tennent Ltd.; music arranged by Lester Lanin; production stage manager, Edmund Baylies. Opened at the Henry Miller Theatre: April 12, 1957.

CAST

Boniface . . . . . . Bert Lahr
Angelique . . . . . . Vera Pearce
Marcelle . . . . . . *Angela Lansbury*
Cot . . . . . John Emery
Maxime . . . . . . Carleton Carpenter
Victoire . . . . . . Sondra Lee
Martin . . . . . . Douglas Byng
First Porter . . . . . . Neil Laurence
Second Porter . . . . . . Mark Lang
Third Porter . . . . . . Fred Baker
Fourth Porter . . . . . . Roy Johnson
Violette . . . . . . John-Ellen Caine
Marguerite . . . . . . Nancy Devlin
Paquerette . . . . . . Patricia Fay
Pervenche . . . . . Helen Quarrier
Anniello . . . . . . Ronald Radd
Georges . . . . . . James Bernard
A Lady . . . . . . Lucille Benson
A Duke . . . . . . Horace Cooper
Tabu . . . . . . James Coco
Police Inspector Boucard . . . . . . George Tyne

A Taste of Honey. A drama by Shelagh Delaney. Directed by Tony Richardson and George Devine; presented by David Merrick, by arrangement with Donald Albery and Oscar Lewenstein Ltd.; scenery by Oliver Smith; lighting by Jean Rosenthal; costumes by Dorothy Jeakins; incidental music by Bobby Scott; production stage manager Del Hughes. Opened at the Lyceum Theatre: October 4, 1960.

CAST

Helen . . . . . . Angela Lansbury
Josephine . . . . . . Joan Plowright
Peter . . . . . Nigel Davenport
The Boy . . . . . . Billy Dee Williams
Geoffrey . . . . . Andrew Ray

MUSICIANS:

Piano . . . . . Bobby Scott
Horns . . . . . . Frank Socolow
Bass . . . . . . Red Kelly
Drums . . . . . Kenny Hume

Anyone Can Whistle. A musical with book by Arthur Laurents, music and lyrics by Stephen Sondheim. Staged by Arthur Laurents; presented by Kermit Bloomgarden and Diana Krasny; associate producer, Arlene Sellers; choreography by Herbert Ross; scenery by William and Jean Eckart; costumes by Theoni V. Aldredge; lighting by Jules Fisher; orchestrations by Don Walker; vocal arrangements and musical direction by Herbert Greene; dance arrangements by Betty Walberg; production stage manager, James S. Gelb. Opened at the Majestic Theater: April 4, 1964. Nine performances.

CAST

Sandwich Man . . . . . . Dick Ensslen
Baby Joan . . . . . . Jeanne Tanzy
Mrs. Schroeder . . . . . . Peg Murray
Treasurer Cooley . . . . . . Arnold Soboloff
Chief Magruder . . . . . . James Frawley

Controller Schub . . . . . . Gabriel Dell
Cora Hoover Hooper . . . . . . *Angela Lansbury*
Fay Apple . . . . . . Lee Remick
J. Bowden Hapgood . . . . . . Harry Guardino
Dr. Detmold . . . . . . Don Doherty
George . . . . . . Larry Roquemore
June . . . . . . Janet Hayes
John . . . . . . Harvey Evans
Martin . . . . . . Lester Wilson
Old Lady . . . . . . Eleonore Treiber
Telegraph Boy . . . . . . Alan Johnson
Osgood . . . . . . Georgia Creighton

Mame. A musical with book by Jerome Lawrence and Robert E. Lee, music and lyrics by Jerry Herman. Based on the novel by Patrick Dennis and the play *Auntie Mame* by Lawrence and Lee. Presented by Fryer, Carr, and Harris; associate producer, John Bowab, directed by Gene Saks; dances and musical numbers staged by Onna White; settings designed by William and Jean Eckart; costumes designed by Robert MacKintosh; lighting by Tharon Musser; musical direction and vocal arrangements by Donald Pippin; orchestrations by Philip J. Lang; dance music arranged by Roger Adams; assistant choreographer, Tom Panko; hairstyles by Ronald De-Mann. Opened at the Winter Garden Theater, May 24, 1966. 1,508 performances.

CAST

Mame . . . . . . *Angela Lansbury*
Vera Charles . . . . . . Beatrice Arthur
Agnes Gooch . . . . . . Jane Connell
Dwight Babcock . . . . . . Willard Waterman
Patrick . . . . . . Frankie Michaels
Ito . . . . . . Sab Shimono
Beauregard Burnside . . . . . . Charles Braswell

With: Jerry Lanning, Margaret Hall, George Coe, Randy Kirby, John C. Becher, Johanna Douglas, Diana Walker, Charlotte Jones, Diane Coupe.

202

Dear World. A musical adapted by Maurice Vallency, based on *The Mad-woman of Chaillot* by Jean Girardoux. Music and lyrics by Jerry Herman; book by Jerome Lawrence and Robert E. Lee. Staged and choreographed by Joe Layton; setting by Oliver Smith; costumes by Freddy Wittop; lighting by Jean Rosenthal; musical direction and vocal arrangements by Donald Pippin; orchestrations by Philip J. Lang; dance and incidental arrange-ments by Dorothea Freitag; production supervisor, Jerry Adler; production staged and choreographed by Joe Layton; associate producer, Hildy Parks; production associate, Roy A. Somiyo; presented by Alexander H. Cohen. Opened at the Mark Hellinger Theater: February 6, 1969. 132 performances.

CAST

Chairman of the Board	William Larson
Board Members	Clifford Fearl
	Charles Karel
	Zale Kessler
	Charles Welsh
Prospector	Joe Masiell
Julian	Kurt Peterson
Nina	Pamela Hall
Waiter	Gene Varrone
Doorman	Michael Davis
Busboy	Ty McConnell
Juggler	Ted Agress
Deaf-Mute	Miguel Godreau
Peddler	John Taliaferro
Countess Aurelia, the Madwoman of Chaillot	*Angela Lansbury*
Sewerman	Milo O'Shea
Madwoman of Montmartre	Jane Connell
Madwoman of the Fleamarket	Carmen Matthews

Prettybelle. A musical with book and lyrics by Bob Merrill, music by Jule Styne; based on the novel of the same name by Jean Arnold. Staged by Gower Champion; designed by Oliver Smith; costumes by Ann Roth;

lighting by Nananne Porcher; musical direction and incidental music arranged by Peter Howard; orchestrations by Elliott Lawrence and Jack Cortner; production supervisor, Jerry Adler; associate producer, Hildy Parks. A Gower Champion Production presented by Alexander H. Cohen. Opened February 1, 1971 at the Shubert Theater, Boston. Closed there March 3, 1971.

CAST

Henry Baines	William Larson
Sybil Mae Asch	Barbara Ann Walters
Prettybelle Sweet	*Angela Lansbury*
Nurses	Susan Plantt
	Linda Lubera
Dr. Dimmer	Richard Kuss
Mayor	Chad Block
Mother Sweet	Charlotte Rae
Lovey Sweet	Renee Lippin
John Sweet	Dean Crane, Jr.
Ray Shaeffer	John Cypher
Willy Thomas	Joe Morton
Cully Hart	Igors Gavon
Huey Lipscombe	Robert Karl
Bubba Rawlings	Jan Leighton
Boy Scout	Brian Hall
Folksinger	Michael Jason
Leroy Sweet	Mark Dawson
GoGo Girls	Susan Plantt
	Linda Lubera
	Chris Cooper
Bouncer	Joe Milan
Pool Hall Mexican	Chad Block
Mason	Peter Lombard
Marie	Chris Cooper
Jesus	Bert Michaels
Motel Clerk	George Blackwell
Bellhop	Bobby Lee
Motel Doorman	Howard Porter

```
              Deputies . . . . . . Chad Block
                                   Robert Karl
                                   Joe Milan
              Magistrate . . . . . . Richard Kuss
      Bud Michaels . . . . . . Sean Walsh
```

All Over. A play by Edward Albee. Directed by Peter Hall; decor and lighting, by John Bury; costumes by Beatrice Dawson. A Royal Shakespeare Company Production. Opened in repertory at the Aldwych Theatre, London, January 31, 1972.

CAST

```
        The Wife . . . . . . Peggy Ashcroft
      The Mistress . . . . . . Angela Lansbury
         The Son . . . . . . David Waller
      The Daughter . . . . . . Sheila Hancock
     The Best Friend . . . . . . Sebastian Shaw
        The Doctor . . . . . . David Markham
        The Nurse . . . . . . Patience Collier
      The Husband . . . . . . Graham Leaman
   The Photographers . . . . . . Colin Edwynn
                                   Vernon Smythe
       The Reporter . . . . . . Godfrey Jackman
```

Sondheim: A Musical Tribute, a musical revue presented for one performance by Kurt Peterson with Craig Zadan and Neil Appelbaum on behalf of the American Musical and Dramatic Academy and The National Hemophilia Foundation, and consisting of the lyrics and music of Stephen Sondheim. Directed by Burt Shevelove; costume coordination by Florence Klotz; lighting by Tharon Musser; choreography by Donna McKechnie. Presented at the Shubert Theatre: March 11, 1973.

CAST

George Lee Andrews	Larry Blyden
Susan Browning	Len Cariou
Jack Cassidy	Dorothy Collins
Steve Elmore	Harvey Evans
Hermione Gingold	Laurence Guittard
Pamela Hall	Ron Holgate
Beth Howland	Glynis Johns
Justine Johnson	Larry Kert
Mark Lambert	*Angela Lansbury*
Victoria Mallory	Mary McCarty
Donna McKechnie	John McMartin
Pamela Myers	Anthony Perkins
Kurt Peterson	Alice Playton
Teri Ralston	Chita Rivera
Marti Rolph	Virginia Sanifur
Tony Stevens	Ethel Shutta
Alexis Smith	Nancy Walker

and

Stephen Sondheim

Gypsy. A musical suggested by the memoirs of Gypsy Rose Lee, with book by Arthur Laurents, music by Jule Styne, and lyrics by Stephen Sondheim. Directed by Arthur Laurents; decor by Robert Randolph; costumes by Raoul Pene Du Bois; lighting by Joe Davis. Original New York production directed and choreographed by Jerome Robbins. Presented by Barry M. Brown and Fritz Holt. Opened at the Piccadilly Theatre, London: May 29, 1973.

CAST

Uncle Jocko	George Moon
George	Stanley Fleet
Clarence	Ludovic Keston
Balloon Girl	Susan Bullimore
Baby Louise	Helen Raye

Baby June . . . . . . Bonnie Langford
Rose . . . . . . Angela Lansbury
Chowsie . . . . . . Honey
Pop . . . . . . Larry Cross
Newsboys . . . . . . Antony Williams
Stephen Proctor
Eric Holliday
Weber . . . . . . John Blythe
Herbie . . . . . . Barrie Ingham
Louise . . . . . . Zan Charisse
June . . . . . . Debbie Bowen
Tulsa . . . . . . Andrew Norman
Yonkers . . . . . . Stuart Locke
Boston . . . . . . Hayden Evans
L.A. . . . . . . Philip Baldwin
Mingo . . . . . . Gerry Tebbutt
San Diego . . . . . . Patrick Reilly
Kringelein . . . . . . Laurie Webb
Mr. Goldstone . . . . . . Stanley Fleet
Miss Cratchitt . . . . . Kelly Wilson
Hollywood Blondes . . . . . . Prue Clark
Rosemary Faith
Beverley Jennings
Jenny Lyons
Heather Seymour
Tara Soppett
Pastey . . . . . . Geoff L'Cise
Tessie Tura . . . . . . Valerie Walsh
Mazeppa . . . . . . Kelly Wilson
Cigar . . . . . . Larry Cross
Electra . . . . . . Judy Canon
Maid . . . . . . Bernice Adams
Phil . . . . . . John Blythe
Bourgeron-Couchon . . . . . . Laurie Webb

Gypsy. A musical play based on Gypsy Rose Lee's autobiography, with book
by Arthur Laurents, lyrics by Stephen Sondheim, and music by Jule Styne.

207

Directed by Arthur Laurents; decor and lighting by Robert Randolph; costumes by Raoul Pene du Bois; choreography by Robert Tucker from the original by Jerome Robbins. Presented by Barry M. Brown, Edgar Lansbury, Fritz Holt and Joseph Beruh. Opened at the Winter Garden Theatre: September 24, 1974.

CAST

Uncle Jocko . . . . . . John C. Becher
George . . . . . . Don Potter
Clarence . . . . . . Craig Brown
Balloon Girl . . . . . . Donna Elio
Baby Louise . . . . . . Lisa Peluso
Baby June . . . . . . Bonnie Langford
Rose . . . . . . Angela Lansbury
Chowsie . . . . . . Peewee
Pop . . . . . . Ed Riley
Weber . . . . . . Charles Rule
Herbie . . . . . . Rex Robbins
Louise . . . . . . Zan Charisse
June . . . . . . Maureen Moore
Tulsa . . . . . . John Sheridan
Yonkers . . . . . . Steven Gelfer
L.A. . . . . . . David Lawson
Little Rock . . . . . . Jay Smith
San Diego . . . . . . Dennis Karr
Boston . . . . . . Serhij Bohdan
Mr. Goldstone . . . . . . Don Potter
Gigolo . . . . . . Edith Ann
Waitress . . . . . . Patricia Richardson
Miss Cratchitt . . . . . . Gloria Rossi
Agnes . . . . . . Denny Dillon
Pastey . . . . . . Richard J. Sabellico
Tessie Tura . . . . . . Mary Louise Wilson
Electra . . . . . . Sally Cooke

Hamlet. A play by William Shakespeare. Directed by Peter Hall; decor by John Bury; lighting by David Hersey; music by Harrison Birtwhistle; fight consultant: William Hobbs. A National Theatre Company Production. Opened at the Old Vic, London: December 9, 1975.

CAST

Francisco . . . . . . Michael Melia
Bernardo . . . . . . Daniel Thorndike
Marcellus . . . . . . Michael Bent
Horatio . . . . . . Philip Locke
Ghost of Hamlet's Father . . . . . . Denis Quilley
Hamlet . . . . . . Albert Finney
Claudius . . . . . . Denis Quilley
Gertrude . . . . . . *Angela Lansbury*
Voltemand . . . . . . Harry Lomax
Cornelius . . . . . . John Gill
Polonius . . . . . . Roland Culver
Laertes . . . . . . Simon Ward
Ophelia . . . . . . Susan Fleetwood
Rosencrantz . . . . . . Oliver Cotton
Guildenstern . . . . . . Gareth Hunt
Reynaldo . . . . . . Peter Needham
First Player . . . . . . Robert Eddison
Player Queen . . . . . . Struan Rodger
Lucianus . . . . . . Michael Melia
Fortinbras . . . . . . David Yelland
Captain to Fortinbras . . . . . . Harry Webster
First Messenger . . . . . . Peter Needham
Sailors . . . . . . Glyn Grain
Peter Rocca
Second Messenger . . . . . . Patrick Monckton
First Gravedigger . . . . . . J.G. Devlin
Second Gravedigger . . . . . . Stephen Rea
Priest . . . . . . P.G. Stevens
Osric . . . . . . Gawn Grainger
Ambassadors from England . . . . . . Daniel Thorndike
Glyn Grain
Gentleman . . . . . . Michael Keating
Lord . . . . . . John Gill

209

Counting The Ways and *Listening*. Premiere performances of two one-act plays by Edward Albee. Producing Director, Paul Weidner; managing director, William Stewart; technical director, Randy Engels; Director, Edward Albee. Presented in repertory at The Hartford Stage Company: September 17, 1976 to June 12, 1977.

CAST

William Prince
Angela Lansbury
Maureen Anderman

Sweeney Todd. A musical with book by Hugh Wheeler; music and lyrics by Stephen Sondheim, based on *Sweeney Todd* by Christopher Wood. Directed by Harold Prince; settings by Eugene Lee; costumes by Franne Lee; lighting by Ken Billington; orchestrations by Jonathan Tunick; musical direction by Paul Gemignani; production stage manager, Alan Hall. Presented by Richard Barr, Charles Woodward, Robert Fryer, Mary Lea Johnson, and Martin Richards in association with Dean and Judy Manos; associate producer, Marc Howard. Opened at the Uris Theater: March 1, 1979.

CAST

Anthony Hope	Victor Garber
Sweeney Todd	Len Cariou
Beggar Woman	Merle Louise
Mrs. Lovett	*Angela Lansbury*
Judge Turpin	Edmund Lyndeck
Beadle	Jack Eric Williams
Johanna	Sara Rice
Tobias Ragg	Ken Jennings
Pirelli	Joaquin Romaguera
Jonas Fogg	Robert Ousely

With: Duane Bodin, Walter Charles, Carole Doscher, Nancy Eaton, Mary-Pat Green, Cris Groenendaal, Skip Harris, Marthe Ihde, Betsy Joslyn, Nancy Killmer, Frank Kopyc, Spain Logue, Craig Lucas, Pamela McLernon, Duane Morris, Richard Warren Pugh, Maggie Task, Heather B. Withers and Robert Hendersen.

A Little Family Business. Adapted by Jay Presson Allen from a play by Barlilet and Gredy. Directed by Martin Charnin; scenery by David Gropman; costumes by Theoni V. Aldredge; lighting by Richard Nelson; sound by Chuck London; hairstyles by Lynn Quiyou; production associate, Harvey Elliott. Presented by Harry Saltzman, Arthur Cantor, and Warner Theater Productions, Inc. Opened at the Martin Beck Theater: December 15, 1982.

CAST

Lillian . . . . . . *Angela Lansbury*
Ben . . . . . . John McMartin
Nadine . . . . . . Sally Stark
Scott . . . . . . Anthony Shaw
Connie . . . . . . Tracy Brooks Swope
Sal . . . . . . Theodore Sorel
Marco . . . . . . Tony Cummings
Sophia . . . . . . Hallie Foote
Vinnie . . . . . . Gordon Rigsby
Joe . . . . . . Donald E. Fischer

TELEVISION

Robert Montgomery Presents, "The Citadel," June 19, 1950. NBC

Video Theatre, "The Wonderful Night," November 6, 1950. CBS

Video Theatre, "Stone's Throw," September 15, 1952. CBS

Robert Montgomery Presents, "Cakes and Ale," October 26, 1953. NBC

Mirror Theatre, "Dreams Never Lie," October 31, 1953. CBS

Ford Theatre, "The Ming Lama," November 12, 1953. NBC

Schlitz Playhouse Of Stars, December 4, 1953. CBS

Four Star Playhouse, "A String of Beads," January 21, 1954. CBS

G.E. Theatre, "The Crime of Daphne Rutledge," June 13, 1954. CBS

Fireside Theatre, "The Indiscreet Mrs. Jarvis," January 4, 1955. NBC

Drama, "Madeira! Madeira!" April 14, 1955. CBS

Stage 7, "Billy and the Bride," May 8, 1955. CBS

Rheingold Theatre, "The Treasure," May 28, 1955. NBC

Studio 57, "The Rarest Stamp," March 11, 1956.

Rheingold Theatre, "The Force of Circumstance," March 24, 1956. NBC

Front Row Center, "Instant of Truth," April 8, 1956. CBS

Screen Directors Playhouse, "Claire," April 25, 1956. CBS

Studio 57, "The Brown Leather Case," June 10, 1956.

Climax, "The Devil's Brook," December 5, 1957. CBS

Playhouse 90, "Verdict of Three," April 24, 1958. CBS

Playhouse 90, "The Grey Nurse Said Nothing," November 26, 1958. CBS

Eleventh Hour, "Something Crazy's Going on in the Back Room," April 3, 1963. NBC

The Man From U.N.C.L.E. "The Deadly Toys Affair," November 12, 1965. NBC

"Little Gloria, Happy At Last," television movie, 1982. NBC

"Lace," five-hour miniseries, September 26, 1983. ABC

"The Gift Of Love," television movie, December 20, 1983. CBS

"The First Olympics; Athens 1896," television movie, 1983.

"A Talent For Murder," television movie, January 13, 1984. cable

Murder, She Wrote, "The Death of Sherlock Holmes" (pilot), September 30, 1984. CBS

AWARDS

Antoinette Perry Award for Best Actress in a Musical:

1966 *Mame*
1969 *Dear World*
1974 *Gypsy*
1979 *Sweeney Todd*

Academy Award Nominations for Best Supporting Actress:

1944 *Gaslight*
1945 *The Picture of Dorian Gray*
1962 *The Manchurian Candidate*

Golden Globe Awards:

For Best Supporting Actress in a Motion Picture

1945 *The Picture of Dorian Gray*
1962 *The Manchurian Candidate*

For Best Actress in a Television Series

1985 "Murder, She Wrote"

National Board of Review of Motion Picture Awards For Best Supporting Actress:

1962 *The Manchurian Candidate*
1978 *Death On The Nile*

Emmy Award Nomination:

1982 "Little Gloria, Happy at Last"
1985 *Sweeney Todd* (PBS version)

Quigley Publications' "Stars of Tomorrow: 1948"

Sarah Siddons Award for Best Actress: 1974 *Gypsy*

After Dark's Ruby Award: 1979 *Performer of the Year*
Elected to Theater Hall of Fame: 1982

RECORDINGS

Anyone Can Whistle. Original Cast. Columbia Records KOL-6080/ KOS-2480. Reissue: Columbia Records S-32608.

Bedknobs and Broomsticks. Soundtrack. Buena Vista Records 5003.

Beggar's Opera, The. Studio Cast. E/Decca D-252D-2. London Records LDR-72008.

Dear World. Original Cast. Columbia BOS-3260.

Gypsy. Original Cast. E/RCA SER-5686. Original Revival Cast. RCA LBLI-5004.

King And I, The. Original 1977 Revival Cast. Private tape, live.

Lady In The Dark. Original Cast of the 1969 Revival. *(q.v. Music Of Kurt Weill, The).*

Mame. Original Cast. Columbia KOL-6600, KOS-3000, and CBS-70051.

Music Of Kurt Weill, The. Original Cast. Private tape, live.

Opening Night At The Winter Garden. Columbia DJ-23.

Prettybelle. Original Cast. Original Cast Recordings, 1982.

Sondheim: A Musical Tribute. Original Cast, with remarks by Angela Lansbury. Warner Brothers 2WS-2705.

Showtime: The Best Of Broadway. Harmony KH-30132.

V.I.P. Night On Broadway. Original Cast. Private tape, live.

SELECTED BIBLIOGRAPHY

Alloway, Lawrence. *Violent America: The Movies 1946-1964.* New York: The Museum of Modern Art, 1971.

Anderson, Christopher P. *The Book of People.* New York: Perigee Books, 1981.

Bordman, Gerald. *American Musical Theater: A Chronicle.* New York: Oxford University Press, 1978.

Brewer, Anne M., ed. *Biographical Almanac.* first edition. Detroit: Gale Research Company, 1981.

Brode, Douglas. *Films of the Sixties.* Secaucus, New Jersey: Citadel Press, 1980.

Brooks, Tim and Marsh, Earl. *The Complete Directory to Prime Time Network TV Shows: 1946-Present.* third edition. New York: Ballantine Books, 1985.

Brown, Gene, ed. *The New York Times Directory of Film.* New York: Arno Press, 1973.

Brown, Gene, ed. *The New York Times Encyclopedia of Film.* New York: Arno Press, 1984.

Campbell, Richard H. and Pitts, Michael R. *The Bible On Film: A Checklist.* Metuchen, New Jersey: Scarecrow Press, 1981.

Collier's Encyclopedia, Vol. 14. "George Lansbury." New York: MacMillan Educational Corp., 1979.

Dimmitt, Richard Bertrand. *A Title Guide to the Talkies.* Metuchen, New Jersey: Scarecrow Press, 1965.

Dimmitt, Richard Bertrand. *An Actor Guide to the Talkies.* Metuchen, New Jersey: Scarecrow Press, 1967.

Eames, John Douglas. *The M-G-M Story.* New York: Crown Publishers, 1985.

Engel, Lehman. *The American Musical Theater.* New York: Collier Books, 1975.

Ewen, David. *The Story of America's Musical Theater.* Philadelphia: Chilton Book Company, 1968.

216

Garbicz, Adam and Klinowski, Jack. *Cinema: The Magic Vehicle: A Guide to its Achievement:* Journey One: The Cinema Through 1949. Metuchen, New Jersey: Scarecrow Press, 1979.

Gertner, Richard, ed. *Motion Picture Almanac: 1983.* New York: Quigley Publishing Company, 1983.

Gottfried, Martin. *Broadway Musicals.* New York: Abradale Press/Harry N. Abrams, Inc., 1984.

Green, Stanley. *The World of Musical Comedy.* Cranbury, New Jersey: A.S. Barnes & Company, 1968.

Halliwell, Leslie. *The Filmgoer's Companion,* fourth edition. New York: Hill and Wang, 1974.

Halliwell, Leslie. *Halliwell's Hundred: A Nostalgic Choice of Films from the Golden Age.* New York: Charles Scribner's Sons, 1982.

Herbert, Ian, ed. *Who's Who in the Theatre: A Biographical Record of the Contemporary Stage.* 17th edition. Detroit: Gale Research Company, 1981.

Hummel, David. *The Collector's Guide to the American Musical Theater.* Metuchen, New Jersey: Scarecrow Press, 1984.

Kerr, Walter. *Journey to the Center of the Theater.* New York: Alfred E. Knopf, 1979.

Michael, Paul. *The Academy Awards: A Pictorial History.* 50th Anniversary edition. New York: Crown Publishers, Inc., 1978.

The New York Times Encyclopedia of the Theater. New York: Arno Press, 1973.

O'Donnell, Monica M., ed. *Contemporary Theater, Film and Television.* Detroit: Gale Research Company, 1984.

Parrish, James Robert. *Actors' Television Credits: 1950-1972.* Metuchen, New Jersey: Scarecrow Press, 1967.

Pickard, Roy. *The Oscar Movies from A-Z.* New York: Taplinger Publishing Company, 1977.

Pitts, Michael R. and Harrison, Louis H. *Hollywood on Record: The Film Star's Discography.* Metuchen, New Jersey: Scarecrow Press, 1978.

Raymond, Jack. *Show Music on Record from the 1890's to the 1980's.* New York: Frederick Ungar Publishing Company: New York, 1982.

Robertson, Patrick. *Movie Facts and Feats.* New York: Sterling Publishing Company, 1980.

Shipman, David. *The Great Movie Stars: The International Years.* New York: St. Martin's Press, 1972.

Stott, William and Jane. *On Broadway.* Photos by Fred Fehl. University of Texas Press, 1978.

Thomson, David. *A Biographical Dictionary of Film.* New York: William Morrow & Company, 1976.

The Video Sourcebook. sixth edition. Syosett, New York: The National Video Clearinghouse, Inc., 1984.

Who's Who 1983. New York: St. Martin's Press, 1983.

Willis, John. *Theatre World.* Vol. 32. New York: Crown Publishers, 1977.

INDEX

ABC, 156
Academy Award nominations, 13, 15
Affairs of State, 41
After Dark, 138
Agee, James, 11, 14, 42
Albee, Edward, 109, 124, 125
Allen, Jay Presson, 150
All Fall Down, 58, 189
All Over, 109, 124, 205
Allyson, June, 21, 41
Ameche, Don, 30
American Musical Theater, 95
American Theater Wing, 8
American Weekly, The, 15
Amorous Adventures of Moll Flanders, The, 74, 143, 191, 192
Anderman, Maureen, 124
Andes, Keith, 42
Andrews, Julie, 110
Antoinette Perry Award, 87
Anyone Can Whistle, 2, 67–73, 78, 111, 148, 201, 202
Arden, Eve, 52
Arkin, Alan, 147
Arthur, Bea, 82, 111
Atkinson, Brooks, 45, 46
Awards and nominations, 1, 2, 13, 15, 29, 86, 94, 121, 136, 138, 156, 213, 214

Bacall, Lauren, 133
Baffa-Baill, Diana, 159
Bagnold, Enid, 13
Baker, Carroll, 75
Baker, Charles Adams, 71, 72
Baker, Kenny, 19
Ball, Lucille, 77, 90, 110, 111
Barnes, Clive, 91–93, 130, 131, 144, 153, 159, 160
Barrymore, Ethel, 13, 31, 34, 35
Baxter, Anne, 51
Beatty, Warren, 58

Becher, John C., 159
Bedknobs and Broomsticks, 98–100, 196
Beggar's Opera, The, 147, 148
Bergman, Ingrid, 1, 11–13
Bernstein, Leonard, 111
Beruh, Joe, 113, 114
Bible On Film: A Checklist 1897–1980, 64
Billington, Michael, 143
Blue Hawaii, 56, 57, 188
Bolger, Ray, 19
Bond, Christopher, 133
Bonynge, Richard, 147
Boone, Pat, 65
Bordman, Gerald, 95
Borgnine, Ernest, 51
Bosley, Tom, 65, 168
Bowab, John, 159
Boyer, Charles, 11, 12
Breath of Scandal, A, 53, 187
Broadway Musicals (Gottfried), 68, 105, 136
Brynner, Yul, 129, 130

Cahn, Sammy, 43
Canby, Vincent, 96, 97, 99, 140, 141
Capra, Frank, 28
Cariou, Len, 133–135
Cassidy, Jack, 111
CBS-TV, 163
Chamberlain, Richard, 30
Champion, Gower, 21, 104, 105
Channing, Carol, 77, 89
Chaplin, Geraldine, 141
Charisse, Cyd, 21
Charnin, Martin, 150, 154
Chevalier, Maurice, 53
Clarke, Graham, 147
"Climax," 212
Cohen, Alexander, 94
Colbert, Claudette, 28, 157
Company of Wolves, The, 172, 199
Condon, Richard, 59

219

White, Onna, 159
Whitty, Dame May, 13
Wilde, Oscar, 10, 14
William Morris Agency, 39, 103
Williams, Billy Dee, 54
Williams, Esther, 19
Wilson, Charles T., 9
Wilson, Earl, 16, 22, 89, 98, 117, 121
Wilson, Liza, 15
Windeler, Robert, 57, 89

Windom, William, 168
Winston, Archer, 147
Winters, Roland, 57
Wolf, Peter, 159
Woodward, Joanne, 49
World of Henry Orient, The, 65, 190, 191
Wynn, Keenan, 34
Wynyard, Diana, 11

York, Michael, 96